Table of Contents

Introduction

Key: Avoid External Definition
- The White View of Race: The Omaha World Herald
- Attempts at Leadership Definition: The Omaha World Herald

Key: Define, at the Outset, What "Empowerment" Is
- African-American Empowerment Network
- Understand the "Politics" of Race and Reality in Omaha: The Conclusions of the 1997 Race Commission Study
- Mentoring: Passing the Baton
- Core Issues: Directions for "Empowerment Network"

Key: Avoid Pacification/Placation Approaches
- North Omaha Community Development
- North Omaha Rebuilding Committee
- NorthStar

Key: Define "Development" In Your Own Image and Interests

Key: Know Your Enemy
- Internal Opposition: Provocateurs and Race Traitors
- External Opposition: Read and Study the Words of Elites
- State of the City Address: Mayor Mike Fahey

Key: Three Approaches to Neighborhood Development?

- Neighborhood Maintenance Approach
- Social Work Approach
- Political Activist Approach

Key: Connect Community Work with "Re-Education"

Key: Define Leadership Types -- Urban Models as a Basis for Black Political Action -- A Theory and Prospective Paradigms

- Concentric Zone Model Community Leadership Paradigm
- Sector Model Community Leadership Paradigm
- Multiple Nuclei Model Community Leadership Paradigm

National League of Cities (2013)

- The Promises of the "Community Partners
- Quotes From the May 15, 2014 Press Conference

Conclusion

References

INTRODUCTION

The area of town known as North Omaha has been the repository for stigma, stereotypes and vitriol from the city – the same entity that "empowerment people" seek to align themselves with - for over a century. A key to understanding the breadth and depth of this citywide belief that North Omaha is not worthy of saving can be summed up by Solomon (1986) where he asserts that, "… stigmas, " ... have a collective quality. That is, in any given social unit, there is likely to be a high degree of consensus about what is considered a stigma" (Solomon, 1986: 65). In this case that social unit is the white majority of Omaha, so much to the point that many black people are even beginning to believe in the negativity.

And Becker and Arnold write,

> Broad views about what constitutes stigma are generally
> shared by members of a society. They will hold common
> beliefs about both the cultural meaning of an attribute and
> the stigma attached to it ... (Arnold and Becker, 1986: 40)

In this case, the beliefs about the central city are shared, and the beliefs about the future of the central city are being projected as being just as negative as the present. Since the same group is in a position to define what is "good and bad" or what is "clean and dirty," then it is clear to me that the future will represent the same stigmatized views of an area that exist in the present.

Even now Omaha's leadership has entered into a "pact" with the National League of Cities, another in a long line of unfulfilled commitments to "help the minorities." In this case it's called a "black male initiative." This will be addressed near the conclusion of this book.

KEY: AVOID EXTERNAL DEFINITION

> Attributing responsibility to stigmatized persons for their
> condition helps to distance an observer from those persons
> and from the stigma itself ... (Gibbons, 1986: 125)

For over a century, the major newspaper in Omaha has worked to define the identity, purpose and direction for black people living in that city. Where many newspapers have altered those tendencies and have indeed, even opted to hire black reporters and columnists, the *Omaha World Herald* hangs on to its conservative mannerisms and tendencies and as a result, remains one of the most racially biased newspapers in the nation.

And yet, this newspaper, which has never had more than three black reporters (out of a staff of more than 60) in its 118 year history, has the gall to write editorials that have to do with "race."

On December 14, 2004, I wrote a response, which included a re-write of the entire original editorial, to the World Herald editorial called, "Interracial Barometer: A Horrendous Assault Brings Reminder of Decline in One Type of Racial Bigotry." What this means is that four or five white men, who form the editorial board, got together and decided that in all their divine wisdom, they were going to shape a social opinion having to do with race. They were going to select the specific subject area and in essence, sit there was judge, jury and executioner (in this sense, the proper word would be "executor").

My response, titled, "The "Barometer" Needs Fixin,' expresses my contempt, not only for the Omaha World Herald editorial board, but for their jejune analyses of history, race and interracial sex (miscegenation).

Following is an essay that contains both the World Herald editorial and my analysis, paragraph by paragraph:

INTRODUCTION
When a newspaper historically known as racist publishes an editorial on race relations, their motives are automatically racist. But in the case of the recent editorial, "Interracial Barometer: A Horrendous Assault Brings Reminder of Decline in One Type of Racial Bigotry," (December 13th) more was displayed that the newspaper probably intended. Following are my views on this article, an article crammed with lies, historical distortions and the World Herald's misinformed manifestations of social reality.

This short analysis of that article should serve as the basis of serious study and discussion regarding media credibility (or lack thereof), the role that race plays in analyzing social issues and, as I taught Tom Shaw several months back, the impact that bias has on editorial boards, most of which are lily-white as is the World Herald's.

The article will also be used as but one more indicator to tourism entities that Omaha is not yet ready to deal with racial diversity.

THE ARTICLE: RACISM AND RELEVANT RESPONSE

Because the Omaha World Herald lacks racial diversity and indeed, uses white women to cover stories in the black community, its journalistic credibility should already be called into question. The fact that they see nothing wrong with this state of affairs is also an indicator of their collective ignorance of race and more importantly, of how the world is changing around them as they apparently opt to stand in place.

The article begins with the following description:

The windows of Joseph Parks' Massachusetts house were smashed. He then was hit in the head, beaten, dragged to an apartment and stabbed in the chest with a knife. Burning cigarettes were placed on him. Racial slurs were written on his back. He was called a disgrace to his race, thrown out of a vehicle and dragged to the railroad tracks. Why? Park is a white man who once dated a black woman.

What was just described has happened to hundreds of thousands of black men over the years. When it happened in the South, the news media avoided printing these stories for the most part. When it happened in Omaha, the news media, led by the World Herald, did the same thing. In other words, the very institution that was supposed to be committed to providing news to the people was selective in what it chose to print. Why? Because of white racism, that's why.

Now we have a white man who has been degraded because of his association with a black woman. But the World Herald doesn't provide context. Was the man killed? Or was this one of those "warnings" that white folks gave their fellow race members for what they called "mongrelizing"? Without informing us of these facts, the World Herald is again showing how piecemeal and partial its reporting and even its editorializing truly is. It makes a big difference if the white man was killed or just beaten badly; it makes a difference how far back the "dating" went and what kind of relationship the two had. Was she his long-time companion? A concubine? A prostitute? What?

With this fundamental truth and contextual set of questions out of the way, journalistic rubrics that even the most defensive and ignorant individual can understand, we can proceed to the following passage:

An appalling story, from which society can take two things. The first is encouragement. Despite the hateful, disgusting display of racism inflicted upon Parks, it's a story that thankfully has become a rare one told over the years.

First of all, the World Herald is in no position to inform "society" about how many things they can extract from a given story. This is ethnocentrism in its purest form: because these white males say there are two points, that is what every reader is supposed to believe? How about readers who have learned to read critically and can therefore think for themselves? It is not their role to tell the reader how many points a story contains: it is their job to present the story for the reader to glean. They could have wrote, "An appalling story, from which society can gather AT LEAST two points." But that would have been too much like real journalism, wouldn't it?

Secondly, the first thing we can take from the story is encouragement. Though Parks was beaten (and we still don't know how severely), we are supposed to be thankful that this story "has become a rare one told over the years."

This is called conjecture. Conjecture is, "Reasoning that involves the formation of conclusions from incomplete evidence." I have already informed the reader of this paper that white newspapers covered up, completely hid or otherwise circumvented stories regarding interracial relationships. So then, how can these nimrods conclude that the race hatred has declined just because the stories have?

As black people, we know about how the white man covers up stories. One white politician who was found dead a few years back was praised about what all he did. What wasn't mentioned was that he was found in an empty North Omaha house dressed in women's clothes. The World-Herald decided they didn't want the public to know. The World Herald itself went out and bought in a polygraph examiner during Hal Daub's mayoral campaign against Brenda Council and they HID the truth but printed what they wanted the public to know. When a black child was used for a Goodfellows campaign a while back, the World Herald changed the gender and race of the child – because THEY felt it was the right thing to do.

So I am making two points here: first, the World Herald's track record disqualifies it from making any believable points regarding interracial relationships when they cover up the ones taking place right here in their back yard and secondly, that their conclusion that such incidents are diminishing is "jive-time journalism" and nothing more than an attempt to appease white suburbanites by convincing them that race relations are "getting better." Racism is alive and, as such, interracial hatred is never going to be "rare." As Fanon taught, "a racist in a culture of racism is therefore, normal."

The article continues:

Gone are the days when a black man was lynched for dating, or even speaking to, a white woman. Gone are the days when interracial couples had to go to court to challenge the legality of their marriages. Gone are the days when the majority of people in this country considered the union of people from differing races as wrong.

The World-Herald's definition of "lynching" is not appropriate and therefore, their conclusion about the diminishing of lynchings is inaccurate. According to the late, great sociologist Oliver C. Cox, in his magnus opus, *Caste, Class and Race*, a lynching takes place any time a group of white men use their numbers and race to attack a single black man. Is this behavior on the decline?

What about crowds of white boys throwing soda on black men at a basketball game? What about the white judicial system ganging up on young black men and giving them time away from their families? What about white cops who single out black men and ram plungers up their asses (Abner Louima case) or gun them down "by accident" as they did Amadou Diallo? In fact, every cop killing is a lynching because it involves a system (white cop is sanctioned) against a lone black person.

It stands to reason that the World Herald would consider such actions on the decline. The newspaper has historically looked the other way when such "lynchings" occur. They did it when Vivian Strong was killed, did it people like Kellin, Ammons, Bibins were all killed by racist cops. None of them had guns. That was a lynching. So when these white editorial writers talk about "declines" they cannot even make that stick here in Omaha, let alone on the national level!

As for the white woman, perhaps the editors should read my 180-plus page response to a recent article that appeared in Newsweek. The Newsweek article was titled, "The Secret Lives of Wives," but it missed so many points I had to respond. In like manner what the World Herald doesn't understand is that the white man has conceded his woman to men of color. He knows what she's about and she's sick of him for the most part. True enough, television and movies don't reflect this reality – yet. But they soon will.

With that understanding, there is no need to lynch a black man for dating or marrying a white woman. That is the white system's way of getting to "Slaves" for the price of one. In many cases she's isolated and shunned and forced to live with black folks. In most cases they both work so the system wins. It's about the money, not about a black man taking one of their blondes away. The fact is, Malcolm X wrote that the act he was most often asked to perform as a pimp was to have sex with a white woman while her husband watched. And this is still going on, right here in Omaha, today. And the World Herald's editors know it all too well.

The issue of interracial couples having to go to court to challenge the legality of their marriages – this was never a major issue or concern. There were widely publicized cases when it happened (again, the media making sure that these cases were publicized, complete with the addresses of the couple involved), but these people knew who was in charge of the courts: the same white boy who is in charge today. The World Herald is grasping at straws in order to buttress its lies. And they should be ashamed.

But the final lie, the deathblow, is where this team of white men claims that the days are gone when the majority of people in this country "considered the union of people from differing races as wrong."

Say what? On what planet are these fuddy-duddies residing? Later, in their own essay, these same men write that, *"Even today, mixed couples are still subjected to disapproving looks, rude comments and silent, yet noticeable, signals of rejection."*

If this is the case, then aren't those looks a physical manifestation that the person doing the looking considers those relationships "wrong"?

But more profoundly, where is the data that supports this incredible fabrication of reality? How does the World Herald know? On what do they base this contention? Because surely, if those days are gone, then gone too would be the days of white people viewing RACISM as wrong! If white people could stop viewing interracial relationships as wrong, this would mean that they would see nothing wrong with the gradual browning of their race.

This would mean that they accept people of color. And this would mean that white racism is on the decline. Anyone who believes that white people are less racist than they were 400 years ago is either naïve about race relations or a total idiot. These crackers are just more afraid now because black people are not as controlled as we were back then. Their fear fuels their racism as much as their hatred did back then. But the effects are still the same: look at the murders of blacks by white cops, look a the prisons and take a long look at the black unemployment rate. Racism has not subsided or decreased; it has merely changed (but not in its intensity).

When those days are "gone," so too will be white folks (as they define themselves today, at least). But once you have a distorted view of social reality (as evidenced in the World-Herald's stories on "black progress" that have permeated its pages this year), any conclusion you arrive at is going to be warped. For example note the following excerpt:

The lack of stories like Parks' is a sign that society has come a long way in its acceptance of interracial unions. But that doesn't mean there isn't more to be done. An impetus for growth also can be taken from this story."

The World Herald again errs, much akin to their earlier perceptual mistake: it is not "the lack of stories like Parks' that is a sign that society has supposedly "come a long way," it is the lack of reporting and media coverage of these stories that is the flaw. The media wants to "play nice" and not report issues of race against interracial couples because it has to take into consideration the city's image, the impact on tourism, the politics of the discrimination, the status of the couple being harassed and so on. The World-Herald knows this: they didn't report those beatings that Daub used to administer to his Asian wife, Cindy, did they?

But even if the World-Herald was correct and the incidents themselves were on the decline, how is this a sign of society coming a long way? This goes back to that white man's thinking that Gunnar Myrdal helped to create in his study, An American Dilemma. All the time the white man felt that what black people wanted was sex with them when, in reality, interracial sex ranked last among the things blacks wanted.

The white man's fears of interracial sex have always been rooted in the way that his mind works: because he raped black women for centuries, he felt the black man wanted to do the same thing to the white woman. This is how the myth got started and the myth, in turn, fanned the hatred that white men had for black people, in general.

Interracial dating and marriage. This was the first thing that those white boys in South Africa "allowed" when apartheid was crumbling. Not more jobs, not better housing, not more liberal policies toward economic development. No. The first thing they said was, "you may now screw our women." Look it up. This contention in itself is racist and a definite put-down of black woman, an issue I will address more thoroughly in a few minutes.

Because the newspaper knows it is lying, it has to qualify its claims that America has come a long way. So they add in the worn cliché, "But that doesn't mean there isn't more to be done." The first thing that should be done is that the World-Herald – along with the rest of the American media – should stop lying. White boys in England still refer to white women who date or marry black men as "slags."

College campuses are filled with white women dating black athletes who have to hear the names they are called in doing so. The campus newspaper doesn't cover these things. The local newspaper, because they need advertisements from the university, don't address it. But just look at who is used to recruit black athletes: white girls. Black people have known this for years. The white man knew, but he was making money prostituting those coeds, so he kept quiet.

These are but a few facts that should show you, the reader, "there is a great deal to be done." There is as much to be done today as there was to be done back in the 1950s, a time the white man dubs, "the golden years." Why were they golden? No black people to worry about. Their sports teams didn't have to compete against us, and white women knew their "place" so the white man had it all to himself. He could act "cool" because there were no brothers to compete against.

But after the Black Power Movement and the Civil Rights Movement loosened things up, white records in sports fell one by one. The white man's control began to falter, and his manipulated "domination" of popular culture disappeared. The "golden years" of the Cleavers of "Leave It to Beaver" and "Donna Reed" were gone. He's tried to relive those times in his movies and TV shows ("Happy Days"), but he knows his time is past. So he pretends as if interracial relationships are more accepted, but offers on evidence to prove it. This is a racist approach in itself: these writers are saying, in essence, "it is true because we say it is so."

These people claim that, "an impetus for growth also can be taken from this story." And what is that? They explain:

It wasn't along ago – 2000 – that Alabama finally removed a law banning interracial marriage (though it hadn't been enforced in years). That same year, Bob Jones University ended its ban on interracial dating. And while society has traveled far in its ability to be open-minded, there still are some people who react negatively when a black man and a white woman, or a Latina woman and a white man, or any other combination, are dating and marrying each other.

You call this "evidence"? One of the most racist states in the union, one that still flies the Confederate flag, decides that it shouldn't be legislating morality and you call this progress? You call it a sign of growth because Bob Jones University ended its ban on interracial dating? You know why they ended it? Because Clinton threatened to take away their Federal dollars, that's why! So once again, the white man had to be bribed to do the right thing in regard to displaying some "humanity."

Having shot down the two examples that the World-Herald office as evidence of "growth," these nitwits with notebooks nevertheless have the gall to claim that society "has traveled far in its ability to be open minded." This has not been established in a single thing that the newspaper has written down. Look at their own city: what is there to point at that shows equitable race relations? The black community is as segregated today as it was in 1950 – the only difference is that the area is larger.

Look at their own newsroom: no blacks in the 1800s and only three in the newsroom today. How can these liars draw conclusions about change when they, themselves, have resisted change? The World Herald, in a hypocritically moralizing tone, writes that "there are still some people who react negatively when a black man and a white woman, or a Latina woman and a white man, or any other combination, are dating and marrying each other."

Few people get angry when a Latina woman and a white man are together because many Latinas have white skin. Unlike the black woman, who is stigmatized, the Latina has the stereotype of the "hot Latin" working for her. Where OWH editors got their information is beyond me. As for a black man and a white woman, this is the most hated relationship by far. Others pale (no pun intended) in comparison.

The twin myths (both concocted by the white man during slavery) of the black rapist and sacred white womanhood still exist today. In another major paper, I look at movies like "The Pelican Brief," "Drive," "I, Robot," "The Bone Collector," and others where a handsome black man is not allowed to be anything to the white female lead but a "friend." This is an extension of the anti-black taboo alluded to earlier.

Those "some people who react negatively"? Guess who most of them are? White males – like the ones sitting in that editorial room writing this bullshit for the gullible Nebraska public to take in. The article concludes:

Even today, mixed couples are still subjected to disapproving looks, rude comments and silent, yet noticeable, signals of rejection. So take some comfort in knowing that most of those who find love outside their race aren't subjected to the horrors that Parks faced. But remember that even one such case is one too many.

Mixed couples? Does the World Herald care enough to provide an operational definition of what they mean? Are they talking about interracial couples? Are they talking about couples from different ethnic groups or religions. Because a "mixed couple" and an "interracial couple" can be two different things.

Furthermore, the editors order the public to "take some comfort in knowing" that "most of those who find love outside their race aren't subjected" to what Parks was subjected to. How does the lily-white editorial board of the OWH know this? Where is their evidence? Are they speaking locally, statewide or nationally?

This brings us to a final point – the title.

How can one incident be a barometer of race relations on any level? How can a "horrendous assault" show a "decline in one type of bigotry"? Even if racial abuse DID decline in that one type of bigotry, would that be enough to offset the institutional manifestations that plague people of color day by day and year by year? Of course note.

When racists like these write about issues of race, they show how little they care by not providing hard data or documentation. They have a preconception about what they want to write about and what they want their conclusion to be. This biased approach is what I tried to tell reporter Tom Shaw about when he made the asinine statement about reporters being "objective" ... The interracial barometer, at least the one that the World-Herald is in possession of, is clearly broken.
And it'll take more than a room full of old white men to fix it.

Never allow external definition of anything that has to do with you, yours or your community. In a city like Omaha, that means having some kind of checks and balances such as the ones I've created: a River City News Council that keeps an eye on the media and its images of blacks; the North Omaha Critique Committee, created back in 1978, and was so shocking to the white mind that it got an article printed in the major newspaper.

Under the headline, "Media Watch By Minorities is Beginning," the article appeared on October 9, 1978:

Several Omahans say they have become "watchdogs" of the media in an effort to ensure equality in the coverage of minority events.

The North Omaha Critique Committee, formed in August, checks the local and national media for items which portray minorities in a negative way, said Chairman Matthew C. Stelly. "Much of what we see, rad and hear in the media is often racist as well as sexist," he said. "Because of the intentional miseducation of minorities, many don't have the chance or the channels to respond to the vile statements leveled against them."

Stelly, a senior at the University of Nebraska-Omaha, said the minority community here has talented writers and< "We intend to use our abilities to expose, correct and rebuke any detrimental images."

30 Members

"What the organization is about is defense of our interests and development of our potential," he said. "These are rights that cannot be given, only exercised." The group's motto is: "To Scan 'The Man' is Our Master Plan."

Stelly said there are about 30 "people of color" in the organization. Each member must subscribe to the World-Herald because "there is no way a person can critique the newspaper by reading it in the library," he said. If members read something they think is derogatory to minorities, they can write a rebuttal which will be submitted to The World-Herald's Public Pulse or Another Point of View.

The person who writes must have a legitimate complaint about something affecting the minority community, he said. Articles must be approved by him or Vice Chairman Jeffrey Patterson before they are submitted.

Focus on Newspaper

"Nobody speaks for the black man better than a black man," Stelly said. Right now the group is mainly focusing on The World-Herald, but radio and TV stations soon will be checked, too, Stelly said.

Plans call for the organization to publish a magazine called "Knocking on the Door." "What we need is a vehicle that will enable us to freely express our feelings about our conditions," he said. The magazine will contain short essays, poetry and some critiques of films and TV shows. Stelly, who came to Omaha from California last year, said there is a similar organization there which was set up by the Pan Afrikan Secretariat. He said the Omaha critique committee "seeks to bridge the gap between the North Side and other communities.

"We realize that much of the polarity around the race issue stems from myths, misconceptions and malicious misinformation. If we can convince one person per day that they have been brainwashed, we will have made an accomplishment that will raise Omaha to a higher level of human existence."

That was 34 years ago, and never really got off the ground because it only existed in my head. But that put white folks on alert, and that is what these "negro leaders" are going to have to do. The key, as I say, is to reject in detail, defiance and self-determination, any image or assertion that is imposed on you by your oppressor. This action is not only defensive, it is also developmental.

Attempts at Leadership Definition: Omaha World Herald

The list goes on and one day the Herald will get its just due. At this point, the most recent contribution to the newspaper's attempt at "leadership definition" can be found in a recent article titled, "New Crop of Black Leaders Eyes New Battles," written by Tom Shaw. Following is my assessment of that article, based upon the realities of what is going on in the black community, the backgrounds of these so-called "new leaders" and the "battles" that the white man says are "new," but which are essentially extensions of the "old battles" against white racism, redlining, job discrimination and racial segregation.

I will break the article down point-by-point and you will see, as I have, what happens white naïve white boys attempt to play the role of "idol maker" in a city as segregated as Omaha, Nebraska.

Now we come to the black leadership issue. The following critical analysis, evidence of how to counter an attempt by a white newspaper to define black leadership, is not an attempt to single out one individual. But in Omaha it seems that the most recent crop of negro leaders is cut from the same cloth: they all seem beholden to the Buffett family and, before that, they were supported by those entities that had a history of doing harm to the black community: Creighton University, the University of Nebraska Omaha Department of Public Administration, Mutual of Omaha insurance, and other white interests.

Therefore, what is being written about Chris Rodgers of the Douglas County Board of Supervisors also fits other leadership (other than politico extraordinaire State Senator Ernie Chambers) perfectly.

First of all, the title: "New Crop of Black Leaders Eyes New Battles." Just the very selection of this title shows that deception is in progress.

For instance, to talk of "new battles" implies that the old ones have been dealt with when indeed, they have not. The "battles" that these people are discussing are battles that, to date, none of them has been involved in. So if they haven't been involved to this point, how are they mystically and magically going to get involved just because the World-Herald, in its most finite wisdom, dubs them "new leaders"? This is the same thing that happened back in 1995 when I foolishly gave Robert Bauldwin a title and some words to say. After a few interviews, he began speaking on his own, which was a big mistake. He told the World-Herald that Triple One represented "the new black leadership" and those white folks, ever watchful of any chance for "divide and conquer," used the term in a headline – just as they are doing now. This brings me to point number two.

There is no need for "new leadership" if it thinks along the same lines as the old guard. With Senator Ernie Chambers as a model and standard, we don't need a bunch of Uncle Toms and Aunt Jemimas shuffling into the picture talking about "bringing people to the table." But I'll deal with that later in this analysis.
The article begins where most white writers like to begin articles that have to do with black folks – casting them in the position of flunky and/or gladiator. In the case of Chris Rodgers, handpicked flunky of Mayor Mike Fahey, it's a combination of both:

> Seventeen years ago, Chris Rodgers thought more about the
> NBA than earning an MBA. A one-time Creighton
> basketball player, Chris Rodgers now appears to be a lock
> for elected office. Rodgers was in the Florence Days parade
> this weekend. Those hoop dreams vanished when knee
> injuries stunted his Creighton basketball career. But instead
> of returning to his tough hometown of East St. Louis,
> Rodgers stayed in school and in Omaha.

Chris Rodgers is a sellout, and has always been one. This goes to show you that even a ghetto as impoverished and crime-ridden as East St. Louis can produce a complete Uncle Tom (some believe that only middle-class upbringings can produce such a phenomenon). But now, the excerpt.

Continuing:

> Last Tuesday, Rodgers, 34, solidified his position as one of
> the city's emerging black leaders when he won the
> Democratic primary for the Douglas County Board. Because
> there is no Republican candidate, he almost certainly will
> serve on the board representing north Omaha. He will join
> other young black leaders who are making their voices heard
> in both political parties and in business.

First of all, how is Rodgers an emerging black leader? He has done nothing for the black community – so then, whom is he leading? Oh, I know: he's a black leader because he has black skin. This is the white man's way of letting "black leaders" know that if they know what's good for them, "blacks" are the only people they better try to lead! What else could it mean? That seems to be all it takes to curry favor with peckerwoods. It also explains why he's considered to be "emerging" as he gets deeper and deeper into a system that white folks control! That is how they define (1) who is a good nigga and (2) who they can trust to assist them in destroying the black community. Rodgers, courtesy of his invisibility, his lack of involvement in key issues, and his lapdog loyalty to Mayor Mike Fahey, has earned his stripes. That's the kind of "black leader" these crackers are talking about.

Secondly, do not be confused: because he was elected to a board "representing North Omaha" doesn't mean that he will be a representative of black people. This is a county position and it has almost as many crackers in it as it does blacks. He will represent white interests, just as his invisible predecessor, Carole Woods-Harris did. She was on that County Board for 12 years and most black people don't even know who she is. She did NOTHING for North Omaha and now, thanks to white manipulation and her endorsement, there is another "do-nothing coon" on the Board: Chris Rodgers.

Third – and most profoundly to this point – is the qualifier and the dupe. You have to be careful because white boys slip in tidbits of fact even as they lie about who YOU should be following and listening to. Check out the following nugget: *"He will join other young black leaders who are making their voices heard in both political parties and in business."*

The logical litany of questions would be, "How are they making their voices heard." Who are they talking to? Who is listening? What are they saying? Then comes the answer: they are making their voices heard in "both political parties and in business" – the two areas where WHITE BOYS HAVE THE MOST CONTROL!!! The two areas where racism is strongest and where the impact of it is most debilitating to the black community and these slackers are supposed to be getting heard? How? Where is the evidence?

Well, here it is:

> While their parents fought to gain equal legal protections for
> blacks, this generation is focused on economic opportunity. "It
> is a different struggle," Rodgers said. "I don't see it as
> somebody who was sprayed with a hose or bit by a dog."

Where is the research to back up this claim that this generation is focused on economic opportunity? Who, besides the ones mentioned in this article, are silly enough to think that you can have economic opportunity without an ideological framework? And what makes Rodgers the "king of blackness"? He knows nothing about his history, which explains his asinine statement about not seeing it as "somebody who was sprayed with a hose or bit (sic) by a dog."

Oh no? Tell that to the family of Marvin Ammons, who was gunned down by a racist cop. Tell that to the family of James Powell, shot in the head in front of his girlfriend on the interstate by a racist highway patrolman back in 1981. Tell that to the family of George Bibins, gunned down by a racist peckerwood who then turned around, got acquitted of the crime and received ding-a-ling ducats (mental disability pay), claiming he (the cop) went nutty following the shooting! Talk about double indemnity!

As an example of how ignorant he is of his own history, check this out. When he was employed at First National Bank, he was such a loser that the white folks contacted one of their richest board members and they got together and created a 'position' for Rodgers. Since the white boy that they contacted had always had some kind of respect for Malcolm X, they created a special fund that would work to promote a Malcolm X seminar and some other crap. They paid

Rodgers $90,000 to head the program. So naïve was he of what to do (after they canned him from the job to give him "more time to work on the project"), he had to contact Dr. Menyweather-Woods at the Black Studies Department and after that, another brother, to ask for assistance. But he didn't want to pay them as consultants: he wanted to pick their brains, steal their ideas, and then pawn them off as his own!

"Black leaders" are not supposed to think – or be able to. All they have to do is be black. That's it. Sit there, smile when ain't nothin' funny and scratch when don't nothin' itch. Agree with the white man when he makes a comment and laugh when he tells a nigga joke. That's their job. And that is why these "leaders" who have been in North Omaha all or most of their lives, have watched as the community has deteriorated: people like Brenda Council, Willie Barney, Ben Gray, Fred Conley, Carole Woods-Harris, Willie Hamilton, and others. Where were those "voices" then?

Then, the writer picks out the few young black leaders who are supposed to represent a "trend" or a "tendency." They begin with Rendell Gines:

> Dell Gines, the 30-year-old new executive director of the
> Omaha Small Business Network, said that in the 1950s and
> 1960s, there were more tangible barriers. "Civil rights gave
> us civil equality, but it didn't give us economic equality,"
> Gines said.

I've know and have worked with Dell Gines a few times. He seems to be a sharp young brother. But as Karenga (1967) wrote, "show me a true nationalist and I'll show you someone who studies." I don't mean "study" because the white man gave you an assignment, I'm talking about reading about your history and culture on your own time; taking life seriously enough to want to improve it, and the only way you can do that is to know something about it!

Gines is what we would call an "involuntary provocateur." He's half-white and is married to a white woman and has six kids. The system therefore knows they've got him. When he was at the job described above, he tried to act black. He tried to get on television and talk like he heard me talk. I tried to warn him that he had too much to lose. He didn't listen, and got canned by some black faggot named Lonnie Mitchell. He's gone from one good job to another, ever since, continuing to act involved in community groups but in the end, dropping out because his commitment is like his skin color: faded.

Furthermore, look at the insipid statement claiming that civil rights gave us "civil equality but didn't give us economic equality." Doesn't this young brother realize that rights cannot be "given," only exercised? Doesn't he know that you cannot be "equal" to a man who owns four houses if you live in his apartments?

Doesn't he know that black people are more than any "equal" of any white man –
and that the white man knows that? This explains why he goes out of his way to
construct those "tangible barriers" that the intellectually bankrupt Chris Rodgers
alluded to earlier.

How can Gines claim that there were "more tangible barriers" in the 1950s
and 1960s than there are today? Those barriers back then laid the rockstrong
framework for the more sophisticated barriers that exist today! Todays are just as
"tangible" but more COVERT, slicker, shrewder and more sophisticated. Why?
Because we kicked their ass with the Black Power movement, not the civil rights
movement! Those white folks didn't respond until we started burning down
buildings and scaring them on the six o'clock news!

Moving right along:

> Several younger black leaders view their role as bringing
> diverse groups together to address issues. Tanya Cook, Urban
> Affairs director for Republican Gov. Mike Johanns, helped
> organize a tour of north Omaha businesses for Johanns last
> week. The setting provided for frank discussion about
> community members' frustrations and how they wanted the
> state to address their concerns. Rodgers and Cook, 39, said
> you can't separate economic troubles from poor school
> performance or health needs. They say attacking all these
> issues at once is key. But to do so, all parties must come to
> the table - citizens, politicians, entrepreneurs and community
> groups.

The idea of bringing diverse groups together is utopian, at best. Here's what
these idiots ought to be doing: *empowering the groups that lack it, and then, once
that is done, everyone comes to the table as power sharers.* In that way, the white
boy doesn't sit at the table as a power BARON; doling out crumbs and
condescendingly participating in a discussion about a community he has absolutely
no knowledge about!

Second mistake: attacking all these issues at once is the key, and that in
order to do so, all the parties must come to the table. The source of the problem is
sitting at the damn table with them, don't they understand that? All they will be
doing is divulging strategy to their own oppressor! The problem is that white man
and his racist tendencies, and as such, the "problems" that exist are not problematic
to HIM! How can someone who has benefited from problems in the schools and
health and economics (do his jails and medical facilities not receive millions based
on black "problems") turn around and reverse that trend? This doesn't make sense!

Third and perhaps most profoundly: what these so-called leaders do is assume that those in power truly have a commitment to change. Where is the evidence that they do? As an example, Governor Mike Johanns recently promised to come back and help black businesses. But he had a chance to show his sincerity level when he visited the Frontier Bag Company. Mrs. Lee showed him the roof caving in and the poor condition of her warehouse. She then handed him an attaché case and asked him if he wanted it. This was his big chance. What did he do? He turned it down. He turned around and left. He could have purchased one; he could have ordered a case of them for his staff or to give away as presents. But he did nothing. And if he didn't do anything when he had the face-to-face chance, he *definitely* is not going to do anything once he gets back to his office in Lincoln.

More ignorance is evidenced in the following statement: "If there's a decision being made that affects you, get people to the table," said L. James Wright, 34, who serves as a district aide to Republican U.S. Rep. Lee Terry.

This "table" that these double-dealers keep talking about is a table that is bought and paid for by their oppressor. They sit back and get happy to be able to sit around it. But what Malcolm X said decades ago still applies today: how can they sit at a table, where the white boys have food in front of them and are eating, and the "black leaders" have no food and no plates in front of them, and still call themselves diners? *They are not diners just because they are at the table!* And this is what decades of brainwashing and degradation have wrought on black people: we are so starved for acceptance that we believe that just sitting at the table is some kind of honor in and of itself!

What do these "black leaders" bring to the table? Problems, complaints, grievances. But even those with ideas are offering ideas that, in turn, will not generate any money for the "diners." Why should those in power educate, clothe and financially enrich those who they oppress? Perhaps these dolts ought to read the Carmichael & Hamilton classic, *Black Power: The Politics of Liberation in America* where it was made most clear: "Before a group can enter open society, it must first close ranks."

But I have a feeling that these black people don't feel comfortable around grass roots black folks. I think these black people would be "embarrassed." I know one of them is totally hopeless – and that's Rodgers. Check out what he told the World-Herald:

> Rodgers has built a lot of bridges during his time in
> Nebraska and met people who have helped shape him. He
> first got involved in politics by joining Bob Kerrey's U.S.
> Senate campaign in 1994 - two years after graduating from
> Creighton with a journalism degree. Rodgers, an aide to
> Mayor Mike Fahey, said Omaha "chiseled and polished"

him. He earned his master's degree in business
administration from Creighton in 1999 and received a
master's degree in public administration from the University
of Nebraska at Omaha in 2002. Rodgers was elected to the
Metropolitan Community College board in 2000. He
married his wife, Sharlon, in 2001.

Omaha 'chiseled and polished' him alright: now he is a nice, new, shiny Uncle Tom! For sale to the highest bidder! Surrounded by racist peckerwoods, cavorting, dining, socializing and when needed, kissing their ass. Running errands, "substituting for the mayor" at those events Fahey couldn't get to, and generally only socializing with other "toms" like himself: Negroes who have titles and no juice.

And he ADMITS he's a "tom" – at least, that's how I interpret the following excerpt:

> Rodgers' style is closer to that of departing County Board
> member Carole Woods Harris than the more outspoken State
> Sen. Ernie Chambers or City Councilman Frank Brown.
> Rodgers called Harris - one of his mentors - a "velvet
> hammer" for her ability to quietly get things done.

Carole Woods-Harris benefited from the hard work of State Senator Ernie Chambers who labored to bring election by district to Omaha. But when it comes to the County Board, you wouldn't know that the black community had any representation. Carole Woods-Harris sat on that board for twelve years and it was as if the seat were empty the whole time! She babbled, negotiated, spoke every now and then – but nothing that had to do with black people. And if this is just what Omaha has gotten from Rodgers over the past three terms he has served, an extension of the same do-nothing approach that Woods-Harris had. Black people won't and don't, benefit.

Secondly, calling one's self a "velvet glove" and claiming that she got things done quietly is nothing but bullshit. The state of black people in Omaha doesn't need people who are "quiet" and "low-key." It needs people who will bring attention to issues, solve problems and then work toward development and defense of the community. But here is the coup de grace that the article is wrapped around: Rodgers likes Harris' style than the approaches of "the more outspoken State Sen. Ernie Chambers or City Councilman Frank Brown."

This was the thrust of the article. White folks at the World Herald working to define leadership – the kind THEY prefer. White men are afraid of black men, for the most part. In politics, they all fear Senator Ernie Chambers. Frank Brown did a good job but Ernie has the experience and the background and the local, national and international accomplishments. What these peckerwoods had to come up with was some "coon" they could use to counter these two. And believe me: they are going to use Rodgers every chance they get. And he will love it. Every time Councilman Brown or Senator Chambers takes a stand on something, the World-Herald will have a reporter "run it past Rodgers." His view will invariably be that of the white man ("What's wrong boss, WE sick?").

Finally, the contrast and comparison sums up the article:

> Rodgers said that he met with Chambers this year and that Chambers told him he doesn't expect Rodgers to do things the same way. While campaigning for the County Board, Rodgers was asked whether he would host a cable television show like Chambers or Brown. Rodgers said he wasn't planning on it. "I would prefer to be more proactive and go meet with people," Rodgers said. He said Chambers and Brown have used television well, but "I don't think I fit into that realm."

Chris Rodgers couldn't do things the same way as Ernie Chambers if you gave him a staff of ten, increased his intellect by 25 points, and a budget of a million dollars. Why? Because he lacks the essential qualities that make Ernie the man that he is: brains, creativity, energy and courage.

Rodgers won't host a cable TV show because the shows are "call-in." He would get dogged every single segment. He knows he's going to be a tom and, up to now, he's been able to insulate himself with white folks: the racists at Creighton, the fuddy-duddies in the Public Administration Department at UNO and Fahey. But now, he's out there on his own sitting on the lily white Douglas County Board, and he can only do what he knows: and that's "Tom"!

If Rodgers would ever get a show on Channel 22, there would be people from all over the community coming to him with their concerns and problems. They would be asking him why he didn't return phone calls. They would ask him to appear in public and talk to black folks. And he would fall way short on every single count. He will use his methods and those of Woods-Harris: laying back, collect a paycheck and save up enough money to run for office the next time around.

Rodgers claims he would, "prefer to be more proactive and go meet with the people." He's never been proactive before. And the only "people" he'll be meeting with are those who are cut from the same bourgeois Uncle Tom cloth he's cut from. That's where he feels most comfortable. And to tell you the truth, that's where he belongs. And he admits as much when he says, "Chambers and Brown have used television well, but "I don't think I fit into that realm." At least he got that much right.

Why this article and why now? When I talked to reporter Tom Shaw on May 17, 2004, he said that he and the editors "kind of came up with it [the idea] together." How this could be, I don't know – unless they were communicating telekinetically. Shaw told me, "We thought that this election was a place to start but we also thought it would be good to include some other voices." When I asked him how he FOUND those voices, he didn't answer the question. The people included in the article were obviously selected by the editors, because Shaw has only been in Omaha for four years.

The fact is, just a few days earlier – Wednesday, May 12th -- Shaw had written an article on Chris Rodgers' victory in the County Board race. It was after this article appeared that these white men got together and decided to make Rodgers' victory a statement on the coming of "new black leadership." In an article titled, "Chris Rodgers Set To Join Douglas County Board," Shaw wrote:

> Chris Rodgers had a solid victory over two opponents in Tuesday's primary election and almost certainly will join the Douglas County Board. Rodgers captured almost 54 percent of the vote in the Democratic primary. With no Republican challengers in the fall, Rodgers is all but assured to win the board seat to represent north Omaha. Opponent Dennis Womack drew about 29 percent of the vote, while Allen C. Johnson had 16 percent.

And,

> Rodgers, an aide to Omaha Mayor Mike Fahey, said he stuck to his message of trying to improve county health and corrections programs. He also attributed the win to connecting with voters. "I just tried to be really sincere about my story," said the 34-year-old former Creighton basketball player and Metropolitan Community College board member.

The fact is, Rodgers eked out a win the an election that had one of the lowest voter turnouts in the history of the state of Nebraska. Why didn't Shaw mention that? Secondly, Rodgers was doing more hobnobbing with white folks than he was talking with black folks. As a result, he makes it sound as if he was in touch with the masses, but that is an inaccurate assessment; he had well-placed campaign signs and posters in North Omaha, but he was invisible for the most part.

These are factors that the Omaha World Herald didn't report because these facts would have gone against the "golden boy" image that they were attempting to paint of Rodgers. This then, would be the story that they would stick with and then elaborate on; using Rodgers and the focus and fulcrum on "new black leadership."

Shaw then asked what I was calling for and assumed he was being interviewed because of my barrage of questions. What I found is that he fits the prototype for a World Herald reporter. He hails from some city 45 minutes outside of Boston, and most black folks know how Boston relates to its black community. Shaw attended the University of Missouri-Columbia, a great school in its own right.

But when we talked about race – which of course, was my intention – he showed an abysmal ignorance of issues of reporter bias. For instance, he said that he doesn't believe that the gender, sex or race of a reporter has any bearing on the story that the reporter is covering! This speaks volumes, not only about his naiveté in regard to race relations, but also about journalism in general: the concept of "objective journalism" was debunked decades ago!

> Rodgers said he'll use the next several months to learn more about county government and the County Board. Carole Woods Harris, who has served as the north Omaha representative for almost 12 years, endorsed Rodgers for the seat. At Rodgers' victory party at the Lothrop Social Hall, Harris said she looked forward to helping orient Rodgers to the position. Harris is running for the State Board of Education. Rodgers will leave the Mayor's Office but said he'll seek another job. The County Board post will pay $26,000 next year. Rodgers earns about $49,000 working for the city.

And so it goes. One last point. Shaw let me know during our telephone conversation that he disagreed with "almost everything" I said, and furthermore, he "couldn't understand" where I was coming from.

That's because Shaw and the newspaper he works for *choose not to*.

Being defined by outside sources and forces is one thing, but being so defined and then refusing to respond means that you've rubber-stamped what has been said, and the public will accept it as true. Even the racist former President Richard Nixon got it right when he asserted, "A man is not finished when he is defeated. He is finished when he quits."

KEY: DEFINE, AT THE OUTSET, WHAT "EMPOWERMENT" IS

For anyone else this would be a no-brainer. If you don't know who you are, then you can't know who your opposition is. And that is the problem with the Network. They chose a word they'd heard before (from me and the titles of the conferences I organized long before they came into fruition) and didn't bother to learn what it meant. I don't mean go by definitions that you got from what your funding sources tell you: I mean take the traditional definition and then shape it in your own image and interests.

Empowerment as it relates to what: making white people more powerful and therefore more in control of North Omaha, or empowerment in the sense of taking existing black institutions (what few there are) and using them to build a power base the way the Triple One Neighborhood Association and Parents' Union worked to do from 1994-2000 (before I left town to pursue my doctorate and other interests).

The name of your organization gives you purpose, identity and direction. Look at the NAACP – National Association for the Advancement of Colored People. Although whites were involved in the founding, black people took control from the outset. The scope is defined ("national"), the orientation is established ("association") the purpose is clearly laid out ("for the advancement of") and so is the major constituency ("colored people," which, in those days, was what Black people were called). The Urban League was founded to help those blacks migrating from the rural south to the city (hence, "urban") and it's orientation was established ("league).

When I created the Triple One Neighborhood Association and Parents Union, I first created a "triple one paradigm" – a model, and then I defined on paper, and then on television in front of thousands of viewers, what I meant. "Triple One" refers to the poorest zip code in the state (outside of the Native American reservations) and that is "68111," in the heart of North Omaha. The neighborhood association meant all black people, however, that is why I defined the boundaries to be all inclusive of North Omaha, also including brothers and sisters from "68110," "68104" and "68131."

Once you have purpose, identity and direction, no one can take that from you. In Omaha the so called leaders involved in recent years appear to have it all ass backwards. They want to call themselves "100 Black Men" (as if they have exactly that number of that this small number is their goal), "100 Black Women" (same problem), and so on. Even back in the day when we were truly courageous, our organizations made it clear what we stood for: Ideal Improvement Club, Mothers for Adequate Welfare, and so on.

When you take a word like "Empowerment" and then add the word "Network," people in the black community think you're talking about helping them by networking with other black people. But that is not what these negroes had or have, in mind. Their network consists of anyone who will give them money, anyone who will claim to be a "partner," and their idea of "empowerment" is to kowtow and cater to the needs of the social order. They want to be all things to all people, "not just the blacks."

For that reason, this paper is important. My views may be in the minority, but they are rock strong and accurate. I'm used to being in the minority when it comes to working with these silly people. As the saying teaches, "You can tell when a genius is on the scene because the dunces immediately form a confederacy against him."

Omaha's version of empowerment is as segregated and divided as its race relations. They have an "Empowerment Network" and then separately, there is an "African-American Empowerment Network." Why would this be the case if the goals are one and the same? You know the answer. The one without a racial designation is the one that is in charge, in control. The one with the prefix "African_American" is defining the scope, content and identity of the group that is to be controlled.

With that having been made clear, let's now take a critical look at Omaha's self-proclaimed "African-American Empowerment Network."

The African-American Empowerment Network

The name of the article that I am about to analyze on the following pages is "Power Players, Ben Gray and Other Omaha African-American Leaders Try Improvement Through Self-Empowered Networking." Other than the obvious lies that the headline conveys, there are a number of additional errors that will lead to clarity once corrected. The African-American Empowerment Network has major problems ideologically, internally, and programmatically. I will now explain why this is the case.

To begin with, "power players" is an exaggeration. None of the men mentioned has any power because if they did, they wouldn't be begging for collaborations with and input from other people, but would be engaging in development on their own. To use that term is Biga's idea: these men know they have no power and would never present themselves in such a way. This is one more example of the white liberal attempting to define issues that do not concern him.

Biga has no idea that using that phrase, "power players" could serve to alienate people from Ben Gray and the others that he has mentioned in his article. He doesn't know how black people think. Black people know that any time a white periodical prints something calling any black man (other than State Senator Ernie Chambers) in Omaha a "power player." All they hear is the word, "player," and based on historical record, black people in North Omaha have been "played" enough, by both white elites and their black lackeys.

The articles begins:

> It may have been 2007 when northeast Omaha's depressed
> African-American community reached its limit. A demographic
> bound by race, history, circumstance and geography seemingly
> exhaled a collective sigh of exasperation to exclaim, "Enough
> already!" Longstanding discontent over inequities in income,
> housing, education, economic development and opportunity
> solidified into resolve by a people to take action.

This paragraph is more racist than the movie "Birth of a Nation," and is filled with nothing more that Biga's uninformed assessments and understanding of race relations and black history. Let me break it down so you will be able to see that not all racists wear sheets or swastikas.

How would Biga know when black people in Omaha reached "their limit"? He says that "it may have been 2007" – where is his evidence. Why did it take so long? Is this must another example of the white man "saying so" and therefore that's the way it must be? As a journalist he offers up not one iota of evidence of how he arrived at this date and how he concluded that the black community had reached its limit. It is all conjecture – racist conjecture.

He adds that blacks are a demographic (he must be talking about black people who, by the way, are not a "demographic" anywhere but on the white man's charts and statistical tables) "bound by race, history, circumstances and geography." But he doesn't say how all this came together. Why is it that black people can be "bound" by all these things and still not produce anything? Why is it that blacks, with all these potentially unifying variables, still remain powerless in a nation where power is valued above all else. Without using the word "racism," Biga and people of his ilk talk of "circumstance," but those circumstances are still dictated by racist decisions made by the people with the power.

Where did this "exhalation" come from? The collective sigh – how collective was it? Was it everybody or just the Christians? Was it a few or the entire community led by the negroes that Biga talks to? Why is he lying and using anecdotes to describe a very serious situation? I'll tell you why: because it's about black people, that's why. And when the subject is black people and North Omaha, people like Biga don't care about diplomacy OR accuracy!

This collective sigh produced the exclamation, "Enough already!" That just happens to be almost the same "slogan" that the negroes put on yard signs and posted all over the black community. The exact slogan was "enough is enough." In the black community we have a saying: "You got to bring ass to get ass." That means you don't say "enough is enough" unless you have something to back it up. And the people that made the signs, like Biga the journalist, are seriously lacking.

"Enough already!," or what? In typical Batman saves Gotham City type comic book hyperbole, Biga claims that the longstanding discontent over various inequities somehow "solidified into resolve by a people to take action." Who were these people? Was it only black people? Was it blacks and their white masters? Where is Biga's information, where are the names, dates and places that could be used to fill in these gargantuan gaps in his historical ignorance?

No matter. It was just a substanceless introduction that led to nowhere. Without mentioning a single name or incident, he then slides from the land of the generic into what the real subject is: the self-proclaimed African-American Empowerment Network. Of that Network, he writes:

> Nearly four years ago, a coalition of local blacks decided to
> rebuild the community from within. They formed the nonprofit
> African-American Empowerment Network. The effort was
> inspired by author and television/radio talk show host Tavis
> Smiley in his best selling 2006 book, *The Covenant with Black
> America.*

Where did Biga arrive at the statement that black people decided to rebuild the community "nearly four years ago"? That would mean that black people didn't deal with this issue until the 21st century! The fact is, I had been writing proposals, essays, news articles, reports, black papers and so on, directed at political leaders at all levels, black people, the ministers and so on, and even coined the term "self-empowerment" as far back as 2003. Where were these "negroes" then? When I was sponsoring community development conferences in the early 1990s, where were these people? The ones whose names you are reading in Biga's document were nowhere to be found.

When I outlined the TripleZip Agenda, a comprehensive plan for North Omaha, did any of these people respond? No. When I laid out "North Omaha 2000" in 1995, as a project of the Triple One Neighborhood Association, did Biga, Ben Gray, Willie Hamilton or Willie Barney come forward with any support? Of course not. Biga's attempt to "date" when black people came to their senses (which most still have not yet done) as being only four years ago is another racist slap in the face of North Omaha.

What is this "coalition of local blacks"? Who does it consist of? And why do these blacks continue to form "coalitions" – which are formed to achieve a short-term goal, and then disband – instead of rockstrong organizations the way Triple One did? And why do black people in Omaha continue to get inspiration from outsiders like the fly-by-night and effeminate Tavis Smiley? How did Biga find out who the source of their inspiration was? And why would these fools admit to the media that their inspiration came from some outsider who, for one thing, has been besmirching the name of Barack Obama just because Barack couldn't attend one of his bullshit sessions and sent Michelle instead? Who does Tavis Smiley think he is?

But this is the kind of leadership that black North Omahans are attracted to. People like George Frazier, a motivational speaker that has no solutions to black people's problems. People like Stedman Graham, Oprah's flunky and another person who is only around for photo opportunities. North Omaha suffers from low-self esteem and believes, like whites in Omaha, that the only good ideas are ideas that come from outside of the area. Tavis Smiley is no more qualified to issue or offer a "covenant with Black America" than a wino is offering up a diagram for a laser gun.

Then jumping forward as if the Empowerment Network's existence is a millennium long and therefore irrefutable, Biga continues his fluff-filled flurry:

> Omaha's Empowerment Network targeted 13 areas for improvement. Efforts by the Network and partners are the latest attempted remedies. In the 1940s and '50s the De Porres Club pressed for civil rights. In the '60s the Citizens Coordinating Committee for Civil Liberties or 4CL, took up the banner. Well into the '70s federally funded programs and agencies spurred by the <u>Great Society</u> and its War on Poverty operated here. At various times the Urban League of Nebraska and the Omaha Chapter of the NAACP have led on social justice and community betterment issues.

What were the thirteen areas targeted and how were they decided upon? Were there any areas that had to do with the racist neglect of the city? Was there the formation of a "liberation lobby" to go regularly to Lincoln to put North Omaha's concerns on the political map? Or was it more of that social work/welfare type shit, where the "13 areas" represent 13 different types of begging from the white man's institutions and where the blacks involved get their palms greased for serving as "liaisons" and "partners"?

Now all of a sudden the Network has "partners." Where did they come from and why can't they just be a part of the Network? I'll tell you why: because they're white and they have power and white people don't want to be involved in any Network where they (the whites) won't hall full power. So they claim to be "partners" and in doing so, they hoard all the resources to themselves and are able to dole out just enough crumbs to the Network to make it appear to be a collective effort.

"Attempted remedies"? Isn't it strange that if you chronicle the history of the entire city of Omaha, the only "attempts" at remedies have something to do with North Omaha? Why are there so many failures? Why so many "oops-we-did-it-again" programs and projects? Because the city, even in its allocations of crumbs, never said that they would spend money on meaningful projects or beneficial programs; they just said that they would "allocate some money." So when that money gets mismanaged, stolen or embezzled by someone, the city doesn't care because they can just sit there and say, "well, ya can't say we didn't try!"

Then the insults continue with Biga reducing the century-plus of black struggle in Omaha to one major incident per decade! He mentions the DePorres Club, which did a lot more than "press for civil rights." It was the DePorres Club, usually chairing meetings at the Omaha Star, that helped highlight housing atrocities and employment discrimination. This is how our history gets trivialized, through white writings such as these.

The fact of the matter is, mid- to late-1940s found increasing numbers of organizations being created that would seek to pressure employers into providing jobs for Black people. One such organization, the DePorres Club, was founded in 1947 by Father John J. Markoe, who had come to Omaha a year earlier. Smith (1980) writes:

> Named after St. Martin DePorres, a Black Latin American
> clergyman, the DePorres Club, although organized by
> Catholics, sought to bring together people of all faiths to fight
> racism. The primary force behind the organization was Father
> John Markoe, a Jesuit priest who was on the faculty of
> Creighton University … Father Markoe considered racism a sin,
> and refused to deal with it gently. His preferred method of
> confrontation, rather than conciliation, and as a result of his
> guidance, the DePorres Club brought to Omaha its first round
> of civil rights demonstrations … (p. 25).

The first meeting of the DePorres Club took place in the home of Mrs. Aleane Carter, mother of Great Plains Black Museum founder Bertha Calloway. According to historian Smith, "in addition to Mrs. Calloway, there was [white civil rights activist and President of the DePorres Club] and Father Markoe. There were also about six or seven Black and White students (Smith, 1980: 76). Jesse Allen, during several major interviews that I had with him, also mentions others, including John Orduna, Herb Rhodes, Sr., John Butler, Richard Turner and Ola McRaney.

According to Eve Hanna, a white woman who was interviewed during an Oral History project, the group, of which she was a member, was organized by people affiliated with Creighton University, and they "conducted many civil rights campaigns. This group broke Coca-Cola and Reid Ice Cream Company because of job discrimination against black people. The DePorres Club was also responsible for winning an important civil rights court decision. The incident involved a 12-year-old Black youth who was refused admission to a swimming pool. The youth was awarded damages of about $200 (Hannah, 1980: 18).

Another one of the early civil rights cases and the court victory that followed, involved a "Mr. Taylor." According to Mrs. Hanna, Mr. Taylor was employed at the Urban League. He was refused food service at the Omaha airport, and the case was taken to court. Mr. Taylor won the decision and was awarded one dollar for damages (Hannah, 1980: 18).

There were some who opposed what the DePorres Club was trying to do in the area of civil rights. But one of the unsung heroes of the DePorres Club was Omaha Star publisher and founder Mildred Brown. When it was rumored that "established negroes" were opposed to the civil rights protest group, the following editorial appeared on the front page of the February 5, 1960 issue of the Star under the headline, "Agitation …" Following is an excerpt:

> Lately some whites and some Negroes (who should know better) have counseled a go slow approach with regard to the many assaults on the rights of Omaha's Negro citizens. Main target of this kind of criticism is the DePorres Club. Some are saying that it has "set progress back" because of its picketing of the Omaha School Administration. These hand wringing do-gooders and some who style themselves outspoken leaders want this paper and the DePorres Club to adopt a head-bowed, hat-in-hand method of commenting on the daily instances of wrong done to Negroes.
>
> This paper is told to speak more softly until "Things can be worked out." We say NO to such suggestions. We stand solidly behind the DePorres Club and its fighting program for arousing the conscience of the people of Omaha to correct the social injustice against the Negro people. Let there be no doubt that we will not shrink from our duty to speak out for those oppressed citizens… (p. 1)

Not to sell the DePorres Club short the way Biga did, recall that also on February 14, 1960, at a conference in Fremont, Nebraska sponsored by the National Conference of Christians and Jews, the DePorres Club ventured forth and presented Governor Brooks with a petition that called for ending racial segregation of teachers and discrimination in the Omaha Public Schools. The organization showed just how organized it was as members distributed handbills during all three days of the conference (p. 1). The group also presented its motto: "Do Something in 1960" to educators who were in attendance.

Biga says that in the 1960s the 4CL – which stands for Citizens Coordinating Committee for Civil Liberties -- "took up the banner," again reducing one of North Omaha's most progressive and productive decades to one group. There was more to it than "taking up the banner." The 4CL bought the community together on major issues, and they also worked for black people regardless of denomination. In fact, they played a major role in bringing Malcolm X to Omaha.

The group was founded during the spring of 1963 by four African American clergymen: Reverend Kelsey Jones, Rev. Rudolph McNair, Rev. General Woods, and Rev. R.F. Jenkins. Again, Smith:

> The 4CL was a grass-roots community organization. While whites were
> never excluded, it was always made clear that the group existed
> primarily to mobilize the black community. Large numbers of people
> turned out for its meetings, as well as for the demonstrations (1980: 27).

The leader of these men was probably Rudolph McNair. McNair was born in Kansas City, Kansas in 1923, the seventh of eight children of Mr. and Mrs. George McNair. His father was a contractor while his mother was a housewife and quite active in the affairs of the First AME Church.

These men were no rookies, but came to the fore with experience. Following his graduation from Sumner High School, the Rev. McNair served five years in the Army, including a two-year European Theater tour-of-duty during World War II as a sergeant-technician. He retired from the Army reserves in 1964. After active military service, the Rev. McNair worked for the government in the post office, Veterans Administration and the Army Reserves. It was a position as a civilian administrative assistant at Fort Omaha's USAR School which brought him to Omaha in 1958.

Rev. General R. Woods was born on June 23, 1909 in St. Louis, Missouri. Woods was a professional musician several years before entering the ministry, and played trumpet, trombone, tuba and bass violin in jazz orchestras (Omaha Star, 1972: 1).

By the summer of 1963, the civil rights movement in Omaha was gaining momentum and respect. The mayor of the city had appointed a Biracial Committee of which Reverend Jenkins said, "Well, I don't think too much of it because it was just a front that did practically nothing, so I paid no attention to it" (quoted in Smith, 1980: 93). (NOTE: The exact same tactic would be employed some 37 years later by Mayor Hal Daub through the creation of a Race Relations Commission. More on that later in this book).

Unlike the Empowerment Network that talks but doesn't get involved in the streets in leading the community, in October of 1963, the 4CL stood all of Omaha on its head when Reverends R.E. McNair and Kelsey A. Jones joined with a number of demonstrators in the City Council chambers and sang and demonstrated during an October 22nd City Council meeting. All were arrested, with McNair and Jones charged with disturbing an assembly (1964: 1).

At a mass meeting of Zion Baptist Church on Wednesday, January 8, 1964, 4CL Vice President told the audience that the group would "increase the intensity and tempo" of their activity during the new year, and that "If the hallmark of our efforts in 1963 was 'Freedom Now,' it will be 'More in '64'" (Omaha Star, 1964: 1). Furthermore, at this meeting,

Furthermore, Biga can only talk about the War on Poverty when it comes to the 1970s, which in reality was perhaps the second most progressive decade in North Omaha's history. For instance, Senator Ernie Chambers got district elections for the Omaha School Board in 1975, and for the City Council in 1979; soul station KOWH came on line in 1972 based on community demands, not individuals the way Biga would interpret it. And what about the fact that in July of 1971, the Black Studies program at UNO officially got its "Department" status? And in 1975, the Great Plains Black Museum became a reality. But all Biga can write about is Lyndon Johnson's "Great Society" concept and the War of Poverty – which, of course, failed.

Biga's research includes some mention of the Urban League of Nebraska and the Omaha chapter of the NAACP, but fails to specifically cite examples. In failing to do this, he lies by *omission.* In playing up the African-American Empowerment Network and their alleged "accomplishments," he lies by *commission.*

But no matter what white man is writing it, they can never leave out the "blame game" to make young people believe that North Omaha is the way it is because of "black riots." The following paragraph is so typical:

> When the last in a series of major civil disturbances in the late 60s badly damaged the old North 24th St. business-entertainment hub, many businesses left. Few new businesses have opened. Northeast Omaha's chronic gun violence contributed to the perception of an unsafe environment. It is regarded as a mission district dependent on government assistance, social services and philanthropy.

What these white people don't ever mention when they discuss how the "riots" tore up 24th Street, is that the businesses that were burned and damaged the most were the ones that were owned by white people and, specifically, Jews. These were the people that had ripped them off for decades, and the riot gave them a chance to get payback. This was not something random – black people knew what they were doing. It wasn't as if they had seen a lot of development money coming down the pike, anyway. White history writers (not historians) like Biga might do well to remember this important fact.

And further, what was the cause of those civil disturbances? Did black people just want to randomly commit acts of vandalism and destruction as whites would feel most comfortable believing? Of course not. What was unique about Omaha is that there were three riots, all of which involved looting and justifiable violence: July 3, 1966 and then another one in August that lasted three nights; March 1968, payback for a racist speech by George Wallace followed by a shooting of 16-year old Howard Stevenson; and 1969, 3 days of looting and rioting following a police shooting of 14-year-old Vivian Strong, killed on June 25, 1969. The physical damage was "payback" by a community that was united in its hatred of racist abuse by the police and the system.

Businesses were lost and few opened, but the ones that did were black-owned this time around. But Biga seems bent on justifying his belief that North Omaha was worthless until the Empowerment negroes came along. Take note where he writes that "Northeast Omaha's chronic gun violence contributed to the perception of an unsafe environment." What chronic gun violence are you talking about? I just showed where those riots were a response to cops gunning down black kids. Senator Chambers has documented scores of cases of police shooting down black citizens. The Omaha Police Division walks around in paramilitary gear as if Omaha was a major city. And yet white writers like Biga make it appear as if it is the black man's use of the gun that is the problem. *The hunter has an entirely different viewpoint when the ducks have guns.*

The perception of an "unsafe environment" is based on the white perception that black people are the majority in North Omaha and that means that is one place where they can't call us "nigger" and get away with it. When they are defenseless and can't flex their muscle, they use the psychological defense mechanism of transference to make the victims appear to be the culprits. Evidently Biga buys into this distorted piece of sociological history.

Then comes another insult and interpretation by the uninformed Biga. He states that North Omaha "is regarded as a mission district dependent on government assistance, social services and philanthropy." The question that he should ask, instead of wasting ink kissing the collective black asses of the Empowerment negroes is, "if this is true, then what made that area so dependent on the government dole"?

Here's the answer before moving on to Biga's next barrage of drivel: if North Omaha became enriched, Omaha would lose almost all of its Community

Development Block Grant funding, which averages about $5 million a year. They would lose most of their Community Service Block Grant money, which goes mostly to ENCAP, a poverty agency. And they wouldn't qualify for the police grants like Weed and Seed and Project Triggerlock. So it's got to remain poor and that's what they do: allow a few to escape through jobs and the rest are there so Omaha can get money from HUD to build "affordable housing" on the fringe of the area to get more to move out. The ones who stay behind will be just enough to constitute that "pocket of poverty" that every city needs in order to qualify for the CDBG money. Does Biga know this, or does he care enough to find out?

Contradictions and game-playing abound and Biga is too blind to see it. Check out the following excerpt:

> President and consultant at Innovations By Design, LLC, Tawanna Black, also vice-chair of the board for the Network, and co-chair for the race relations covenant, summed it up. "In the absence of African-Americans in powerful political or economic positions to drive this, small changes have occurred but nothing major. The Network really flips that theory on its head and says,"Why are we waiting for the power to be given? Let's own the power that's within.' It's an empowerment thing. It means more than just a name on a piece of paper. It's really what it's all about empowering people to take control of themselves. A process committed to that is completely new in this community."

Tawanna Black doesn't know anything about black people. She's married to a white man and owns a boa constrictor, and doesn't even live in Omaha. She was bought in for who knows what reason, but since she's arrived she's had some powerful jobs. They put Ms. Black in charge of a Midtown project where Mutual of Omaha and others lied about being a blighted area so that they could receive Tax Incremental Financing. Now they've got shops and businesses surrounding the district, a hotel and movie theater, all of this with Mutual of Omaha as the hub.

Why would the Network have a "race relations covenant?" Let them tell it, everything is just peachy-keen when it comes to race relations. If the Network is interracial, why would there be such a need since their "target" is North Omaha? This is nothing more than window dressing, akin to the "race commission study" that was conducted in 1997. Who is going to sign a covenant on race relations? This is as shallow as former President Bill Clinton's "apologizing" for slavery. The apology, like the covenant, is only the beginning. My question in both cases is this: where are the financial reparations for the decades/centuries of abuse?

If Ms. Black knows there is an absence of African-Americans in powerful political or economic positions, then shouldn't job one be trying to locate or develop some? Of course not because this would challenge the status quo – white folks in charge, even when it comes to black-oriented projects. So what do they do in terms of "flipping that theory on its head"? They say the very same things that I have been saying since 1977 – turn our power inward. I even provided them with a model: the Triple One Neighborhood Association and Triple One Parents Union. They watched and saw what I was able to do with these two groups, representing the families and youth of the "68111" zip code (hence, "triple one"), the poorest zip code in the state of Nebraska.

Then Ms. Black says, "let's own the power that's within." How sophistic. If there is no power then what are you going to own? What she should be saying is let's develop our power potential from within our own ranks. What did Stokely Carmichael and Charles V. Hamilton write more than 40 years ago? *"Before a group can enter open society it must first close ranks."*

Furthermore, by stating that "we must own the power within," this doesn't challenge the status quo, once again. As long as white people have the real power, these negroes are willing to concede that and then try to "own" something somewhere in the black community, then report back to the white man with their findings. You what this kind of person was called back in the day? An overseer. The only power the overseer had was over the enslaved folk out in the field, and other than that, he was nothing but a flunky and snitch for the white man.

Is this the kind of "power" that people like Tawanna Black want to own?

What she's saying about empowerment is really self-empowerment and I've got three consecutive conferences to back up the fact that I've been talking about this concept since the beginning of the 21st century. So when she says that" a process committed to that (self-empowerment) that is completely new in this community" is an outright and absurd lie.

People who don't study look stupid when they try to make socio-political statements or draw up plans. I've proven that throughout this paper, from the writings of Leo Biga and the World Herald to negro leaders in North Omaha, having been duped into thinking that they have "juice." More evidence lies ahead. For instance, note the following:

> "There's been a lot of psychological damage done to us as a
> people. Historically we just allow things to happen to us and
> what we have to do is starting taking control of our own destiny
> and that means also having skin in the game," said Omaha City
> Councilman and Network violence intervention-prevention
> chair Ben Gray.

When Ben Gray was the director of the African-American Achievement Team, very little was achieved other than a so-called "greeter's program." Now he's supposed to be the chairman of the Network's "violence intervention-prevention" committee. Since violence has not been quelled or addressed in any major way, this means that he has, once again, failed. How can you "prevent violence" without developing internal programs that deal with the subjective and material conditions? Once again, if this Network did that, they would have to call white folks on the carpet and they don't have the courage to do so – the hand that feeds, controls.

Gray, who probably never enrolled in a Black Studies class while a student at UNO, has the gall to try to sound like he knows something about the black psyche. He makes a general statement that is true about the psychological damage and then turns around and puts is foot in his mouth by claiming that, "Historically we just allow things to happen to us and what we have to do is starting taking control of our own destiny and that means also having skin in the game."

How silly. We're not psychologically damaged because we "allowed things to happen to us." Those things happened despite our resistance to them. His statement smacks of those foolish beliefs that black people submitted to slavery. Nothing could have been further from the truth. When there were efforts afoot to take control of our own destiny, I was present when Ben Gray personally used the microphone and his control of it to turn those efforts back. He's turned those efforts back everywhere he's gone. He's one of the reasons why white folks are so deeply involved in the business of the black community.

Then he says that we have to have "skin in the game." What "game" is he talking about? If he's talking about the race situation in Omaha, this ain't no game. And perhaps the key to his on-going failures are revealed in his statement about having skin the game. Do you know what that means? It mean's just being there; it means just sitting at the table and saying nothing. It means just breathing while other people plan and talk. Skin just means you exist. Karenga (1967) wrote that, "Membership in the black community requires more than just physical presence." Having "skin in the game" is Ben Gray's philosophy (the terminology was recently used during a speech by New Jersey Governor Chris Christie) on community development because when he just sits there he's probably getting paid by the opposition. I say if you go to a meeting and nobody knows you've been there, you wasted your time and everybody else's as well.

Jargon. Clichés. Possibly some old rap lyrics. *Anything to quote rather than some coherent strategies for struggle*. For instance,

> Empower Omaha drafted a rising-tide-lifts-all-ships community
> covenant. Through monthly community meetings, periodic
> summits and prayer walks, neighborhood cleanups, block
> parties and surveys, the Network interfaces with residents
> through a North Omaha Neighborhood Alliance.

"A rising tide lifts all ships." "Pick up the bottom of the barrel and everything in it is lifted by extension." "A stitch in time saves nine." "A bird in the hand is worth two in the bush." Good Lord, man! Don't these people see how stupid they look? Ten years from now if anybody reads that newspaper and Biga's article, they are going to scratch their heads and ask, was everybody in the Network retarded or on the pipe? Because that's sure what it sounds like.

Not a coherent thought or logical plan among them! They just meet, choose up sides as if they're about to play a game of kickball, give themselves some titles and that's it! Ten years from now will North Omaha be any better off? Probably. Ten years from now will North Omaha black people be any better off? No way! This is not about black people hunkering down and turning their power inward. That was already being done before the white man interloped into the area back in the early 1960s (a point that even the sophistic Biga will acknowledge). And from then it was downhill. We had a few spikes during that time, but those were periods when black people reacted to situations, discrimination and neglect and scared white folks into doing something.

Look at their "strategic plans:" prayer walks, periodic summits (meaning meetings among themselves), neighborhood cleanups, block parties and surveys (why survey the obvious? The need is starting you straight in the face!). This is why white people laugh at us behind our backs. This is why Omaha is an invisible blip on the map of major cities. This is why so many black kids are getting the hell away from that town and heading elsewhere. This is why there is a brain drain among all young people because the maltreatment of North Omaha is so obvious and glaring, even white kids can't take it anymore.

And yet these people talk about planning for the future? And then, even in the midst of their buffoonery, they have the gall to make statements such as those which follow:

> "We keep the community engaged, we listen to the community,
> we write down what they say. I think that's how we get the buy-
> in from the community," said director of operations Vicki
> Quaites-Ferris. "Most things implemented actually come as a
> result of listening to the community."

These lies are being shared with Biga because the people telling them know that this white man couldn't know the truth. It's a fluff piece, an interview being conducted by a race relations novice. So they lie. This woman, who is director of operations, would not make these statements to a black publication of any merit because the community would read it and know that she was lying.

For instance, what "community" do they keep engaged? How do they engage them? What have they done besides the neighborhood watch, block party stuff mentioned earlier? Has the community become so engaged that they (the Network) would not be needed in, say, three years? That is the goal of a good organization that is out to uplift a community: to put itself out of a job. If they did their job, the community that is so "engaged" would eventually become empowered.

They claim they listen to the community. Does the community even know when the meetings are being held? Why would you write down what "the community" says in this day and age of tape recorders and video cameras? Where is the evidence that the community has bought in to what the Network is doing? Was there a survey? Is there a support list? And when she claims that most of the things that have been implemented (like what?) have been a result of listening to the community, then I have a question: of what good is the Network? If the community has the ideas and is so engaged, then the Network is reinventing the wheel and should disband. As Judge Judy says, "If you tell the truth, you don't have to have a good memory."

Next come contradictions and as a result, more confusion:

> Highlander Neighborhood Association president Kristina Carter
> said the Network's an integral part of neighborhood cleanups.
> Network strategies encompass neighborhoods, housing,
> employment, education, family, faith, crime, etc. The strategies
> come from community leaders, residents and best practices in
> other cities. Not a direct service provider, the Network partners
> with others to support or facilitate programs.

When my neighborhood association – the Triple One Neighborhood Association and Parents' Union – was one of seven neighborhood groups statewide to win the "Project of the Century" award from the Urban Community Improvement Association, Highlander was one of the other six. During that time they were opening up learning centers after school for young people and were doing an adequate job in that area.

I don't recognize the name Kristina Carter, but I do know that Highlander did a lot more than just clean up the neighborhood. And if the Network is an integral part of these cleanups, then they are simply re-inventing the wheel: this is what the Ideal Improvement Club was doing back in the 1940s (along with other community activities). Then all this other stuff is added regarding housing, neighborhoods, employment, education, family, faith and crime.

Here's what I want to know: where is the evidence of Network involvement? What are they doing in terms of affordable housing, helping with rent and so on?

What are they doing in the area of education, since black kids in the Omaha Public Schools are having major problems? Where is evidence that they are stabilizing and/or assisting with the defense and development of black families?

Nowhere to be found. That's why in the next sentence Ms. Carter states that the Network is "not a direct service provider" but indeed, "partners with others to support or facilitate programs." So I ask again, of what good are they? This so-called "Empowerment Network" is not about empowerment: it is a social service liaison, a referral agency – a middle man. They have no power to provide direct services but that is what the masses need: direct relationships with those who claim to be their leaders. Instead, they farm the work out to whom? Social Services? Workforce Development? Family Housing Services? This may be necessary, but it is not sufficient – especially when you are playing around with and mouthing platitudes regarding "empowerment." How can you empower others when you, yourself, are lacking power?

As stated, I was having Empowerment Conferences every year, from 2001-2004. None of these people attended a single one of them. I gave out awards, fed the community, and had the event at the Omaha Opportunities Industrialization Center, in the heart of the black community, so the people would know that Triple One didn't just talk and try to lead by proxy: we were directly involved in the bread and butter issues that impacted their lives.

Knowing this, check out the following attempt at an explanation to get "dibs" on empowerment and show a (feigned) concern about the condition of North Omaha:

> The Network was in place before a 2007 Omaha World-Herald series revealed black Omaha poverty rates as among the nation's worst. What was already known is that many youths underachieve in school — only half graduate. There is an epidemic of sexually transmitted diseases, a preponderance of single-parent homes and little economic development or opportunity. Newly detailed were high jobless rates and low household income levels. Freeway construction disrupted, some say severed, a tight community. As restrictive housing practices waned, upwardly mobile blacks moved west. Others left the state. Many feel the city needs to make an "It stops here" pledge.

Again, it is imperative to blame North Omaha for its plight, blame the residents for their condition. If not, the only other choice would to be to blame the white people whose decisions and neglect led to the negative demographics that the Empowerment Network is constantly citing.

If the Network was in place before the poverty rates were released, then why didn't they know about the rates beforehand? The key to leadership is information, or don't they know that? You would think that a group that is essentially nothing more than glorified social workers would at least understand social dynamics.

So after citing Omaha's high ranking in black poverty, one would think that the inevitable follow up would be for this group of "leaders" to outline why that was the case. What are the socio-political, financial and educational factors that led to these statistics? No, not the so-called "empowerment" negroes. They immediately allow Biga the reporter to jump into dogging out the kids and talking about under-achieving in school, about low graduation rates. That's Ben Gray's area as the leader of the so-called African-American Achievement team. Doesn't look like much "achieving" is taking place, does it?

Then, another right cross: not only are the kids being blamed for not having any brains but they're also responsible for the spread of STDs! Then there are the single-parent homes which are also our fault, and very little economic development or opportunity. These are two different things: economic development is the result of a plan; opportunity is a human right. The fact is, white folks have been in control of both these areas which explains why the community is deteriorated and why opportunity – except for a few well-placed negroes – is non-existent.

The article claims that a preponderance of joblessness and low housing income levels are "newly detailed." Bullshit! As far back as *The State of Black Omaha Report, 1978*, statistician Manny Martinez documented not only low housing income, but also median housing value and a plethora of other issues that were overlooked in the subsequent reports that would appear over the years, many of them co-opted by the University of Nebraska Omaha's Center for Applied Urban Research (lot of good they've done over the years).

So far the article by Biga, with the blessing of the Network, has managed to blame the black community for the condition it is in. There has not been one mention of any improprieties on the part of the city or the state and the entities that are supposed to be addressing the problems of that area. There is not a single mention of Senator Ernie Chambers who has bought this information to the fore long before the Urban League report of 1978 did it. This is a fluff piece. It is poor journalism. And the Empowerment Network, based on the statements of its self-proclaimed "power players" appear to be nothing short of a group of loquacious quislings.

The Network was in place before 2007, evidently didn't read any of the State of Black Omaha reports, evidently didn't see black men getting shot down by cops and black prostitutes being propositioned by the same; they evidently didn't see or hear what I had been laying out, idea and proposal by idea and proposal, for North

Omaha's uplift. When and how did they get on the scene? What are their community credentials?

Biga – with the Empowerment Network's blessing –continues to lie and distort the social history of North Omaha. For instance, he writes that "freeway construction disrupted, some say severed, a tight community." Where were the Network people when Senator Chambers and I were bringing together the UNO campus and the community to oppose that roadway? The ones who are saying that the freeway severed the community were shouted down by the same white people that the Network now caters to and hobnobs with. One of those persons is now Mayor, and his name is James Suttle. More on him in a minute.

Biga, in his incredible ignorance of urban planning and Omaha history, comes to the conclusion that "restrictive housing practices waned" and "upwardly mobile blacks moved west." If these housing practice waned at all, it meant that they existed at one time. And if they existed at one time then what prompted them to "wane"? The economy! The attitudes behind the practices didn't wane, though. Black people moving out to west Omaha did so as renters and those who purchased homes ran into more racism: redlining, steering and over charging by area banking interests. Why didn't Biga mention that?

And what is an "upwardly mobile black"? Does he mean those with good jobs? Because good job or not, if you were black in Omaha in 1970 you still could only live in North Omaha or face ridicule and harassment by those suburban white folks. And as reliable studies show, those who move out west do not cut their ties with North Omaha, because that's where they have to go to get hair cuts, go to the beauty shop, get their nails done and visit family and friends. Biga is, once again, confusing *appearance* with *essence.* This is what happens when you don't do your homework.

He adds that, "others left the state." Why would that be? Why doesn't he write, "others left the state because, while more than qualified, they simply could not find work in a city as racist as Omaha." This statement is far closer to being the truth than what he wrote. He makes it sound like black people were cowardly and "hatted up" because they couldn't take the pressure. What he is describing are the actions of cowardly white people and a concept known as "white flight." Again, he should be consulting urban planning scholars: no other race could stand the abuse and humiliation that black people have had to undergo simply in order to eke out a quiet existence in a segregated ghetto. That's not because of the lack of courage; that's because of the pre-eminence of white racism.

As a result of all of these "observations," what does Biga come up with, and what do the negro leaders endorse? "The city needs to make an "It stops here" pledge." What is "it"? Racism stops here? White women cruising the community looking for young black bucks stops here? Liquor stores all over the community stops here? Abuse of federal funding that should be getting spent on north Omaha but instead is spent on parks downtown stops here? Silly white boys acting like they know something about the black experience and expose their ignorance in writing stops here?

What is needed is more than a "pledge." Do you know what a "pledge" is? It is "a solid promise or agreement to do or refrain from doing something." Would this pledge be legally binding? How would it be enforced? What would prompt the city to pledge to do something that would cost it billions of dollars if they did, indeed, stop "it"? Making a pledge is a gesture or a symbol and most pledges are made to be broken and are shallow – as in the "Pledge of Allegiance" which is filled with lies that you are supposed to believe actually exist. Why would people with no morals make a pledge and expect others to believe it? This is the best that these people can come up with.

I have an idea: why doesn't the so-called "Empowerment Network" make a pledge to stop cavorting with the enemies of the community and selling North Omaha acre by acre? Why doesn't it make a pledge that you can't be a part of the Network unless you live in the community that is being impacted?

Biga hand picks the black people he talks to, which is why he interviews people who are both safe and lacking in knowledge:

> Rev. Jeremiah McGhee doubts the larger community yet
> appreciates a revitalized north Omaha is good for all of Omaha.
> The city has managed a united front against gun violence. The
> Network has endorsements from Mayor Jim Suttle, Omaha
> Police Chief Alex Hayes and some 100 public-private partners
> for the Omaha 360 anti-violence coalition.

How did Biga find Jeremiah McGee, a so called "reverend"? The word on the street is that this guy marries young couples and links the wedding to some kind of voodoo rituals. I don't know if it's true or not, but this much I do know: he's a sellout and will do anything for a buck. But then, this is the kind of black person that Biga is comfortable around. It's almost as if he (Biga) has some kind of "bootlicking sixth sense." He knows not to mess with Ernie and when he asked me about an article, I told him to get lost (and a few other choice words).

The point here is that the preceding excerpt features McGee and then it makes a reference to "Mayor Jim Suttle." This is the man who helped spearhead that freeway that was mentioned earlier, remember? He was the one who lied and did whatever he could to get the money to force that freeway through the heart of North Omaha. Remember? And now here is the Empowerment Network aligning themselves with him. "The friend of my enemy is my enemy."

I don't know the police chief, but he was black, and now he's retired. All I know is that when you align yourselves with cops, what you're doing is ingratiating yourself to them. You helping them to harm our kids in most cases. These people want to befriend cops so that the cops won't arrest them when they come staggering out of one of these bars or commit an act of domestic violence. They turn our kids over to them, and they trust them. These acts, in themselves, should show the true character of the Empowerment Network.

And that so-called "Omaha 360 anti-violence coalition" is a joke.

For one thing, 100 public-private partners are just signing on because how could they not? What do you say when someone calls begging you to be a partner to "stop violence in North Omaha"? Well, you're white and you know the blacks are violent so you say, "sure, I'll help." So now you can become a partner. No response on letterhead, nothing in writing, no contract "pledging" that you'll put in work. Just a claim that, "I'm in!"

And check out the name, "Omaha 360." Do you know what a 360-degree circle is? It means you've come full circle. So they start out without a plan and not knowing what to do and that is where they end up. That is what the name implies, does it not?

Biga continues editorializing, but the contents of what he says (not the manner in which he writes it) also shows complicity by and from, the Network:

> Connecting the dots, it became clear that despair is rooted in
> certain realities: entrenched gang and drug culture; fractured
> families; a lack of positive role models; barriers to educational,
> job, home ownership and business opportunities; a sense that no
> one cares.

Connecting what "dots"? What a foolish concept: when you're dealing with social issues it's not about connecting dots, it's about developing a plan and then approaching the collective problem using an ecological (contextual) approach. Evidently the Empowerment Network doesn't know this. When you connect dots from one problem to the next, all that does is reinforce the stigma that already exists: the problems (dots) are the result of black people's inability to "get with the program." Nothing could be further from the truth.

That connecting the dots concept and the addition of the word "despair" reminds me of the "cycle of despair" that Weinstein and Fantini wrote bout in the middle 1970s in their book, *The Disadvantaged*. It was just another way of dealing with the so-called "cycle of poverty" and admitting that there were no solutions. But of course there are solutions, but they are rooted in undoing the cycle, first and foremost! At the base of the problems that are mentioned is the white abuse of the system and the racism that is a part of dealing with the black community in the same way that you deal with blacks on an individual basis: with disdain-and-how-dare-you.

Then Biga (and the Network, by extension) believe that despair is rooted in what they call, "certain realities." He's listed them, but let me regurgitate them and I'll include what I believe to be the source or basis of each of these "realities." At no time does he mention the fact that the "realities" are rooted in a designed plan and intention of the white majority in the city of Omaha.

Entrenched gang culture: How did the gangs get to an "entrenched" status? The gangs are here because the kids who are involved in gangs live in North Omaha. So the kids are entrenched because they're trapped in a situation where they realize they live in a city that continues to abuse, neglect and deprive their parents. The source of gangs: bad police work and low-income status.

Entrenched drug culture: The drug culture is entrenched because everybody is taking some kind of drug. Within North Omaha alone there are about five Walgreen's Drug Stores, and there are also CVS Drugs and other "pharmacies" including those at Baker's and Albertson's (Save-On Drugs). As for street drugs, the need for them is obvious when life-chances are sabotaged. North Omaha has been a "social experiment" for decades, and the drugs came in, just as they did in Los Angeles, as a tool of control. The source? A drug culture that wants to distinguish between "prescribed" drugs and "street" drugs although in many cases, the residual effect is the same.

Fractured families: It's easy to blame single-parent families for problems that are actually community-wide. The other agents of socialization available to young people include the schools, the media and their peers. These families are not "fractured" because the extended kin and pseudo-kin networks more than compensate for the absence of a parent in the home. Source of the problem: The media and social work view that the family is the problem, a tangle of pathology, a cycle of despair and so on. All these, in combination, lead to internal, psychological and behavioral manifestations of "despair."

Lack of positive role models: If the individuals who make up the Empowerment Network consider themselves role models, then THAT seems to be a cause for despair, not any LACK of them! The problem is that what the decision makers consider "positive" may not be all that positive in the eyes of young people. Politicians who take bribes, get caught gambling away more money than a black family of four earns in a year, people on TV hobnobbing with the policymakers who debase the community, these are the people being pawned off as role models. What is the source of the lack of positive role models: a definitive statement on what constitutes "positive." When black kids see the media and black and white politicians insulting Senator Ernie Chambers – the only man they respect – this only makes them want to further reject the people who are claiming to be "positive role models." You have to be a man or a woman first – that's an ascribed status. A role model is an "achieved" status and the people whose names have appeared in this paper have not done that. They are "dubbed" positive role models by the people who aren't affected.

Barriers to educational opportunities: In Omaha, the barriers are the fact that there are no opportunities for the black child to learn about himself. The curriculum is lily-white and the only time blacks are mentioned is as slaves or during civil rights discussions. Add to that the fact that black kids are more likely to be placed in EMH classes than in Gifted and Talented, and it is clear that the decision makers are creating the obstacles. Blacks in OPS fare so badly that few can pass the entrance test given out by nearby University of Nebraska at Omaha and may be getting "steered" to Metropolitan Community College, a 2-year school in the heart of North Omaha.

Barriers to job opportunities: The main barrier to job opportunities in Omaha is the lack of transportation. Want proof? The data from 1990, taken from the 1990 census, gives us an idea of the differences between black and white relationships to the issue of transportation when the context is the city of Omaha:

Table 3. Transportation access by race

Mode of Transportation	Omaha MSA (whites)	Northside residents (Black)
Automobile	86%	70%
Carpooling	12%	19%
Metro Area Transit (bus)	2%	11%

SOURCE: 1990 Census/Chart by Uhuru Sasa Research Institute

Furthermore, Omaha's black community is a place where, in 1978 it was reported that fully 45% of residents lacked automobiles (Urban League of Nebraska, 1978: 20). Five years later nothing had changed. According to an August 7, 1983 article in the Omaha World Herald documented that, "Nearly 45 percent of the households on the Near North Side have no cars. So residents walk or rely on taxis, buses or rides from neighbors and relatives to get to stores along Ames Avenue or shopping centers to the west."

Barriers to home ownership: What is the source? To begin with no job which as I say, is related to and rooted in the lack of transportation (and of course, job discrimination by white decision makers). Black home ownership has decreased, even since the 1920s. Want proof? Take note of the home ownership ethic that was observed in a December 14, 1928 editorial in the *Omaha Monitor* newspaper:

> There are some features about Omaha that perhaps we do not
> appreciate as we should. Among these should be mentioned
> the largest percentage of home-owners. It is stated upon the
> authority of real estate men that 30,000 of the homes in this
> city are owned by them that live in them. Omaha has 51,000
> homes, and 30,000 of these, think of it! More than 60 per cent,
> or three out of every five of the homes in this city, are owned
> by the occupants. This is a record unequalled by any other
> American city. We can point with commendable pride to the
> fact that Omaha holds the record for home ownership. And it
> is noteworthy that our own race contributes to this splendid
> record, the estimate being that 45 per cent of the Negroes are
> home owners (Omaha Monitor, 1928: 2).

Across the nation black people are facing "obstacles" (mainly the banks, job discrimination, etc.). For example, according to the *2002 State of Black America* report, 2002,

> Compared with whites and the rest of the nation, blacks are
> still stuck in the pre-civil-rights era when it comes to
> owning their homes. For whites, homeownership rated is 74
> percent. For blacks, it is 48 percent – the national rate in the
> 1940s (Omaha World Herald, 2002).

More recently, Edney (2004) documented that, "within the African-American community, less than 50 percent of U.S. citizens are homeowners, compared to 70 percent for whites" (p. 11). Home ownership among black people in North Omaha has actually decreased since 1928! The outcome is described, but the "reality" lies at the door of a system whose banks, other lenders and discriminatory real estate representatives work in cohesion to manipulate where and how black people live. This then, is the source of despair, even in the face of the fact that so many black people are so desperately trying to achieve an American Dream that is really, as Malcolm X said, an American "nightmare."

Barriers to business opportunities: Here are the facts that Biga came up with (probably provided to him by someone black and then he omits the source so that people will think that he actually engaged in some research): *"A recent Pew Partnership for Civic Change report found that of 33,000 metro businesses, only 200 are black-owned – most are single owner-operator endeavors."*

And that's the way it was in Milwaukee as well: most businesses have one employee and that one employee is the owner. So what is the Omaha Small Business Network doing? It was charged with assisting with the start up of small businesses. What is the City of Omaha doing with the CDBG funds that were supposed to assist, not only through OSBN, but as a primary venture, to help provide jobs and opportunities for residents of the "pocket of poverty" as they call it? Therefore what is the source of the barrier? Who controls the economics? Who controls the allocations processes? Who performs intake and the application process? It's surely not North Omaha's blacks.

A sense that no one cares: This is nothing but anecdotal foolishness. If despair is rooted in a certain reality, and that reality is that no one cares, then explain this: where are all those Christians who are sitting in Salem Baptist Church, Zion Baptist Church, Mount Moriah Missionary Baptist Church, Pleasant Green, Paradise and all those other institutions every Sunday? If the Empowerment Network just got with the program in 2007, then what would they know about a sense of not caring on the part of residents that they have very little contact with or concern about? Where have they been all this time?

Where is the evidence? For over a century black people have believed that somebody cares about them. Now here comes Biga, listening to numbskulls, who want to believe that the issue is that there is despair because black people don't think anyone cares. The issue is that black people know that the city administration doesn't care, and that is the source of the problem. These people are a small minority of the population but they hoard the power and decision making. The Network, as I've stated earlier, is simply comic relief, window dressing and "affirmative action" evidence that the otherwise lily-white city is doing it's "garsh-darndest to help the negro people."

In absence of a plan and an historical understanding of the situation, the pity party for North Omaha by those who claim to be leaders, continues:

> Douglas County Treasurer and Network chair John Ewing
> knows it from his former career as an Omaha cop and
> Empowerment prayer walks and community meetings. He said
> residents complain of violence, lack of economic opportunities,
> that they feel abandoned, neglected, overlooked, forgotten. It
> leads to a sense of hopelessness. And northeast Omaha's lost
> some 11,000 households over time. A diminished tax, voter,
> consumer base diluted the minimal clout it had to hold public
> and private sectors accountable the economic and social ills.

Prayer walks. This man was a cop, and he didn't do anything to stand up for the black community. No one really even knew who he was until he ran for public office. Now that he's not a cop he wants to act as if he's some kind of civil rights leader. It is difficult to know where the words of black people end and where Biga's editorial meddling begins. At any rate, the following statement is shared: "He [Ewing] … said residents complain of violence, lack of economic opportunities, that they feel abandoned, neglected, overlooked, forgotten. It leads to a sense of hopelessness."

This is how it was planned. Do you think that white people would be letting these kids run all over the place shooting guns if the guns weren't aimed at other black people? Of course not. Do you think these white people would be allowing housing stock to deteriorate unless they had a long-range plan? Of course not. All of these feelings – neglect, abandonment, being overlooked, forgotten – these descriptors beg the question, "So what? Where were you?" These feelings are not new? What did you do about it when you were a cop?

Some 11,000 households were lost "over time." How much time? Over a decade? Over 5 years? Since the 60s riots? How long. Households were lost but that doesn't mean that they're not still in the area. They were lost, not to Omaha, but to that particular demographic. These are people that moved to another zip code or area. These are people who are among those that Biga claims moved to west Omaha. When you say that someone or something is "lost," you owe it to the reader to explain why it was lost. Households don't disappear on their own.

More gloom peddling leads the writer and his negro friends to claim that, "A diminished tax, voter, consumer base diluted the minimal clout it had to hold public and private sectors accountable the economic and social ills."

The tax based is diluted because of all those damn churches in North Omaha! Every time a nonprofit sets up, that means that no taxes go into that structure and that means less money for area schools. There are a total of 458 churches in Omaha and 116 of them are in North Omaha. What does that say? So before you start looking to the stars and some chicken-eating preacher to save you, just think about the fact that every nonprofit program, agency, organization or entity in an area further deprives that area of the taxes that a for profit business would be paying in.

Voter base? What does that have to do with accounting for economic and social ills? Since when have politicians and elected officials cared about North Omaha. I am of the mind, looking back, that black people in North Omaha were better off before Senator Ernie Chambers fought for, and got passed, the district elections format. The piss-pot poor leadership that we've had since then, especially on the City Council and the Douglas County Board, is so weak, mealy-mouthed and uninvolved that I don't think that at at-large election producing a white man could have done the community much worse. At least we could lay some white guilt on a few members of these boards and win some concessions. But with black people like these in power, we have to deal with white racism on the outer ring and "buffer negroes" on the inner ring.

The consumer base would not make or break the area because ever since "integration" came, black people have shared their shopping priorities between white store owners in North Omaha and white supermarket owners on the fringe and beyond. The supermarkets that do serve North Omaha charge more for the food and offer lower quality and less options. The consumer base, according to the Greater Omaha Chamber of Commerce, in 2004, Black people in Omaha had a total purchasing power of $593 million dollars. That was eight years ago and the figures are probably either about the same or lower. But that's still a powerful chunk of money not to be spent in the area where you live. Those who have transportation go where the sales are and for the most part, that's Wal-Mart, Baker's, Albertson's and No-Frills.

Now these various "bases" – tax, voter and consumer – didn't dilute the minimal clout that the area had to hold public and private sectors accountable for economic and social ills." Biga has been attempting to read an urban economics text and doesn't understand that these principles essentially do not apply to black communities and their relationship with the white power structure. As I have shown in my brief notes earlier, voting doesn't work because the people we vote for do not see our community as a priority. Taxes are cut because of the proliferation of nonprofits organizations. And the consumer base, when provided with options, is smart enough to go where they can get the biggest bang for their buck. Small stores have to charge more because they cannot afford to purchase in bulk the way large supermarkets can. So if you had a shopping choice, which would you use?

Ben "The Apologist" Gray is always good for "explaining away" issues that defend the powers that be (witness his quotes to the National League of Cities at the end of this book) . His ancient and almost decadent views on social reality would be laughable if not for the fact that Omaha is filled with black and white people who are so gullible that they believe what he says. For instance, take note of the following:

> "There's been a lot of benign neglect that's gone on in north
> Omaha by the majority community and I don't hesitate in saying
> that because it's a fact," said Gray."But what we've got to do
> now is rather than point fingers and place blame put together the
> necessary mechanism to fix it. We've got so much work to do
> and we've got so many areas that we're operating in."

Benign neglect. This is a term that was popularized by former President Richard Nixon during his term. And it meant paying little attention to black communities just the same way that Ben Gray does today. So one the one hand its prophetic and on the other hand, pathetic. More specifically:

> Benign neglect was a policy proposed in the late 1960s by New York
> Sen. Daniel Patrick Moynihan, who was at the time on Nixon's White

> House Staff as an urban affairs adviser. While serving in this capacity,
> he sent the President a memo suggesting that "the issue of race could
> benefit from a period of 'benign neglect'. The subject has been too
> much talked about....We may need a period in which Negro progress
> continues and racial rhetoric fades." … However, the policy was
> widely seen as an abandonment of urban (particularly black)
> neighborhoods … (Wikipedia, 2012)

So if there is any "benign neglect" taking place, it's on the part of the Empowerment Network! They are the ones who minimize the impact of race; they are the ones who avoid "racial rhetoric;" they are the ones who have abandoned urban neighborhoods and essentially turned them over to white developers and the city of Omaha. Ben Gray's words speak volumes – but not in the way that he thinks.

And he acts as if he says something that is profound and confrontative when, in reality, it is flattering to white people. How? The neglect that black people have been victimized by has not been benign – it has been malignant! The definition of "benign" in this case, is "showing or expressive of gentleness or kindness." How is the city's neglect, after intercepting hundreds of millions that our poverty qualified them to receive, even close to being "kind" or "gentle?" The term "benign neglect" was coined to cover the ass of a man who hated black people. Now the apologist, Ben Gray – who will do whatever it takes to support the system -- is doing the same thing.

He sounds just like the white man who is saying, "patience is a virtue" or another one of their pacification favorites, "let's forgive and forget." Now that they've stolen everything and have black people in various forms of servitude it's time to do, just Gray said, "rather than point fingers and place blame put together the necessary mechanism to fix it. We've got so much work to do and we've got so many areas that we're operating in." And that is why the Empowerment Network is a reactionary and anti-black entity: they all believe that the system is the solution and that black people ought to forget the past and move on to a future that is guided and directed by the same white folks that tried to destroy the community in the first place. Their track record speaks for itself.

One step out of slavery, two steps back into it. That is the goal of the next "power player" who is one of the key developers of this "Network." He is a man whom I respect very much and I sat across the table from as he explained what his purpose for the Network was. That purpose has evidently changed. According to the article by Biga,

> Davis Companies CEO Dick Davis spearheads a formed
> Economic Strategy Taskforce whose goals address economic

> viability. Those include preparing every African-American for a
> sustainable living-wage job; moving persons from
> unemployment or underemployment to full employment and
> from jobs to careers; encouraging entrepreneurship by
> increasing access to credit and capital. The Network endorses a
> from-birth-to-career strategy.

Within a limited context such as Nebraska in general and Omaha, in particular, just how much of a strategy can you develop? When Davis and I met, I gave him a list of national foundations, locations and deadline dates for applications. This was a strategy: to go outside of Nebraska and use Davis's business background to solicit funding from outside. He must have totally disregarded my work and, in fact, his own initial goals (at least, as they were explained to me). Let's look at the preceding excerpt and count the conceptual errors in logic.

To begin with if you're at the point where you've formed an Economic Strategy Taskforce, your goals have got to be more than just addressing economic viability. Viability of what? The community? The financial climate? The people that you want to employ?

Then the goals that are listed are not goals in a climate like Omaha's: it's more of a wish list or a list of "ideals." Goals, for one thing, have to be attainable and realistic. Check out these goals outlined by Dr. Davis and let's see how realistic they are.

One of the goals is, "preparing every African-American for a sustainable living wage job." How do you do that? Don't you mean every "qualified" black person? And if that is the case, then what kinds of living wage jobs are you talking about? Will the jobs match their qualifications or are you just trying to get them into the workforce? How do you define "sustainable?" Nebraska is a right to work state and as such, thousands of black people have been "let go" for a number of reasons because the workforce doesn't even have to have a reason.

Another goal is to "move persons from unemployment or underemployment to full employment and from jobs to careers." How will that get done? Will employers allow this to take place? How will this impact on those who are receiving pensions or some kind of aid – they are only allowed to earn so much money on a job, right? Before a person is moved from unemployment or underemployment, shouldn't there be some kind of transition program to prepare them for returning to the workforce and having to interact with or deal with people who may have "attitudes" about race?

A third "goal" is "encouraging entrepreneurship by increasing access to credit and capital." This means "special arrangements" with banks and other lenders because the "encouragement" is going to have to be backed up with something. Furthermore, increasing access to credit and capital is not enough: its gaining or getting your hands on that credit and capital that is the best "encouragement," is it not. We've always had access to these things, but it was the same kind of access that a homeless person has to walking into the Ritz Carlton; you might walk in, but that don't mean you're gonna make it to the front desk!

As evidence that these well-meaning "goals" are really nothing more than an idealistic wish list, take note of the fact that, "The Network endorses a from-birth-to-career strategy." How can you endorse a "from birth to career" strategy when along the way, you will be confronted by and with institutional arrangements that may not be in your corner, from schools and the media to the cops and the courts? Furthermore, why "birth to career"? Why not make it from birth to the grave?

And furthermore, why a career? Unless that place you work has your image and interests at heart, all a career ends up being is a lifetime of indentured servitude! There's a difference between a job and a career. If you want black people to have a career, make it something that is about helping other black people. As one cultural nationalist taught, "If you are black, your purpose is to build black" (Karenga, 1967). A career is defined as, "an occupation or profession, esp. one requiring special training followed as one's life work." If Davis can get people long-term jobs, that's alright. But a career means you're dedicating your life to what you do. Who wants a career as a janitor or a grave digger? It's jobs that black people want because most black people don't want the responsibility that comes with a career. They love white people so much that just to receive a paycheck from a white company is their ultimate goal. Careers, like these ideals set forth by Dr. Davis, are dreams.

Moving right along:

> Davis has long been active, starting black businesses and
> providing college scholarships to black students. Entities like
> the African-American Academic Achievement Council, 100
> Black Men, 100 Black Women, the Omaha Economic
> Development Corporation, the Urban League of Nebraska,
> along with black churches, have done their part. Pockets of
> progress have appeared in some new home construction, a few
> business parks, a refurbished section of North 24th St. and new
> quarters for anchors Salem Baptist Church, the Urban League
> and Charles Drew Health Center. Nothing large-scale has been
> attempted.

None of the groups mentioned really do anything for the community as a whole; none of them understand the importance of the ecological approach. They carve out a little niche and even their names are insultingly narrow in their goals and vision. What white group would call itself "100 White Men" or even "100

Men" for that matter? Why limit yourself by a number? I've never heard of "100 Black Women," but it figures that a group like that would pop up in competition with black men. What about "100 Black People"? The separation of the genders is one reason why we remain fractured and fragmented when it comes to the need for collective struggle. White women support their men in upholding the racist system; we want to knit-pick about how we respond to it.

Two of the groups above – the Omaha Economic Development Corporation (OEDC) and the Urban League – have no real track record working with the entire community. The Urban League, having gotten away from housing and employment, is really nothing more than a glorified social service agency, first under the corrupt George Dillard (17 years as director) and now under ex-police chief Tommy Warren. OEDC is the group that the city uses as its "negro pawn" when it comes to tiny development projects, most of them irrelevant except for small pockets here and there.

What does it mean that these groups have "done their part"? Why not elaborate on exactly what these groups are doing, because it's a fact that the majority of black people sure don't know. Some of them target young people and claim to be mentors, while others, as stated are into social services and referrals. But none of them is about the community as a whole. And as we know, *to divide the process is to deform the product.*

And what is a "pocket of progress"? Progress is not a static essence – it is on-going. How can you call it a pocket of progress and then cite "some new home construction, a few business parks, a refurbished section of North 24th Street,, and new quarters for anchors Salem Baptist Church, the Urban League and Charles Drew Health Center? Furthermore, most of this "progress" took place in the middle 1990s, so what Biga is doing is mixing different "happenings" and trying to make it look like a consistent on-going plan when it is not.

They mention Salem Baptist Church. Since when did they do anything for anyone but their own coffers and congregation members? Salem Baptist Church? Salem Baptist Church benefited from the North freeway's intrusion. In fact, Salem was one of the structures that was initially relocated. The church building and the land it was on was sold to the City of Omaha for $150,000.

> The Rev. J.C. Wade, then the church's pastor, said, "It was like losing a loved one to some of us. Some of the people grew up there, but they've adjusted well." Two other area churches were forced to move as well. (Trandahl, 1972).

The money generated from the sale of the church enabled Salem leadership to purchase the land and build on a new location, 3336 Lake Street, in the heart of the black community. Estimates on the value of that structure range from $350,000 to $425,000.

By the early 1990s, Salem was talking about expanding, even though it was already the largest church in North Omaha. The church purchased the huge space on the southwest corner of 30th and Lake Streets, left behind when the Hilltop Projects were torn down in the summer of 1996. The $4 million church, which is now standing, boasts some 50,000-square feet. As one 1996 article reported,

> The Salem Baptist Church, which was established 75 years ago, has been discussing for about three years the need to expand. Its current church is at 3336 Lake St. – about a block from the Hilltop site. There are about 2,500 members, Watson said, 650 of whom can sit in the sanctuary at any one time. In the last eight years, Salem's membership has grown 50 percent, said Watson. "We don't project that kind of growth is going to slow down." Salem Baptist ministers to the "whole person," Watson said, which includes serving social and educational as well as spiritual needs. He said a larger facility will help the church better meet the human needs of north Omaha. "We want this to be an anchor of the community," Watson said (Gonzalez, 1996: 2).

So Salem had moved from a place where people met to oppose a freeway to being the beneficiaries of the sale of property that paved the way for the freeway. Now with its new church atop a hill on 30th and Lake Street, Rev. Maurice Watson claims, "We pledge to make the Hilltop property the most beautiful and productive area in north Omaha," and added, "We will transform what once was a repository of despair, drug abuse, crime, gangs and violence into an oasis of hope" (Gonzalez, 1996: 1).

The project even had the backing of the Omaha World Herald. In typical "manipulate black leadership" fashion, take note of how the major newspaper pumps up a project which, at that time, existed only on paper:

> There ought to be an extra spring in the performances of the Stepping Saints, the drum-and-dance corps from Salem Baptist Church in Omaha. That's because there is good news indeed in the Salem Baptist community. The 75-year-old congregation has announced plans for a new church and school on the site of the former Hilltop Homes low-rent housing project.
> "An oasis of hope" – that's what Rev. Maurice Watson, pastor of Salem Baptist, called the proposed $4 million campus. The campus would offer physical education and social programs as

well as worship services and education. The 16-acre plot is on
the south side of Lake Street, between 30th and 33rd Streets.
  The project would benefit Salem Baptist. It also **should**
help bring stability to the surrounding neighborhood.
  Watson said the current church, about a block west of the
proposed new site, seats 650 people. With membership
growing 50 percent over the last eight years to 2,500, Watson
said, Salem has been looking to expand.
  The new campus also seems to fit the Omaha Housing
Authority's plan. OHA owns the property and has been
working on a plan to restore vitality to the section of Omaha
immediately east of 30th and Lake. That target area would be
well-served by the enhanced presence of Salem Baptist as a
community resource center.
  How heartening it is to see a venerable Omaha church stake
out a bold course for the future. Federal and local officials
ought to move quickly to facilitate the sale of the site to Salem
Baptist. **Close the deal** and let those saints go stepping as
proudly as ever into the next century (Omaha World Herald,
1996: 6—emphasis added).

Even the world Herald saw that Salem was going to be the sole beneficiary.
Note where the article says that the project SHOULD help bring stability to the
surrounding neighborhood. White people know that churches don't turn
communities around – economic development does; retail outlets do; banks and
other financial "anchors" do. Not churches. So where does the World-Herald get
the idea that this religious institution – which takes money from the congregation
but gives nothing financial back – going to stabilize an entire neighborhood when,
since its congregation members are there for help and salvation – it can't even
stabilize THEM??!!

No sooner did they purchase the property than did Salem decision makers
sell a chunk of it to Walgreen's and now, to the east of the church on the hill sits a
new Walgreen's Drug Store. And contrary to what was promised, the area
surrounding the "church on the hill" has actually deteriorated and those
"programs" that were being promised and bandied about have yet to materialize in
the year 2012 – fifteen years after the earlier pledge was made.

The reason why I spent so much time sharing information about Salem
Baptist Church is because it is the foundation for how the Empowerment Network
got started. So this says a lot about how the product would be formed: it is a
church that doesn't get involved in the important issues of black people and, in
like manner, the Empowerment Network – despite the easily assembled lies of
Leo Biga – seems to have the same method of operation. More on the Willie

Barney/Empowerment Network/Salem Baptist Church connection in a few minutes.

So Biga takes projects from the mid-1990s and mixes them more recent activities (while naming none) and makes it appear as a "pocket of progress." What Salem did to benefit itself is the same thing that all the rest are doing: running to the white man, hat in hand, and claiming to want to "stop the violence" if they can get paid for it. Progress?

Total confusion, as I charged earlier. According to the article Teresa Hunter – another nearly invisible "leader" that Biga somehow dug up – serves as co-chair of the Network's housing development covenant, said "We work within the framework of what's already going on, trying to make it cooperative … Why are people still falling through the cracks – what else do we need to do?"

Why was this statement even left in the article since all she does is show that she doesn't know which way is up? And yet, she is the director of an agency that is charged with locating housing for people who need it. This is not the exception – it is the rule when it comes to North Omaha negroes.

The article about "empowerment" continues on:

> Where most Network players are native Omahans like Hunter, the driving force is a transplant, Willie Barney, who until recently was a strategic consultant. The Iowa native worked in media marketing for Lee Enterprises and moved here for an Omaha World-Herald post. He worked on Salem Baptist Church's administrative team when he galvanized efforts to create the Network. He served as the Network's unpaid president and facilitator, then as a consultant, and is now its second paid staff member.

"Network players"? Did these negroes give Biga permission to refer to them in such a way? Is this an abbreviation for the "power player" lie that was a part of the headline? Most of the "driving forces" behind anything in the black community are transplants. But if he's from Iowa, he's not a real transplant: a hick is a hick. Not only that, but he worked in media marketing and when you look at his contributions to black life in Omaha, that's about all you'll find: free publicity, free marketing, free public relations – whether deserved or not.

Then Barney jumps from the pan into the fire by moving to Omaha to work for the Omaha World Herald. I did the same thing when I arrived in Omaha: I typed the want-ads for the World Herald and learned everything I could about racism in Omaha and at the newspaper from Rudy Smith, the only black in the photography department and Sibyl Myers, the only reporter on staff. Of course Barney would join up with Salem Baptist church because the negroes in Omaha are quick to point out that Salem is the biggest and many (not all) say that it is the oldest black church. In addition, that is where all the bourgeois negroes who think they're special attend church.

Now Barney is a paid staff member. What is the source of their revenue? How much is he being paid? Is this some of that Suzie Buffett money? Is the source somehow linked to the city of Omaha? What are their fundraising and long-time economic development plans to sustain the organization? Remember what I've been saying: the hand that feeds controls. How can you be about "empowerment" when your very financial base is one of dependency and reliance on the same system that has worked to destroy the community that you purport to want to protect?

> "In evolving over time we've stayed true to our mission," said Barney. "We said we want to be positive and pro-active and to build partnerships … with the entire city. It has to be bottom-up and top-down for it to be anywhere close to being successful — individuals, families, leaders at all levels working together collaboratively."

What does this have to do with North Omaha? You heard it from his own mouth. He said that they want to be positive: sometimes in order to obtain a positive result you have to be willing to tackle the negative, like for instance letting these white people know that what they're doing is not charity, but a form of "reparations" for more than 100 years of neglect and discrimination. But the Empowerment negroes don't have the guts to do that because it would be threatening their funding source.

Barney says they want to be pro-active, but if you want to be proactive you have to have a direction and a philosophy. To be proactive is "serving to prepare for, intervene in, or control an expected occurrence or situation, esp. a negative or difficult one." So the problem is the abuse of North Omaha and the people responsible for it are not North Omahans. So in being proactive, Barney and those of his ilk would have to be prepared to address a situation that is negative – meaning discrimination, segregation and racism. But they cannot do that because they are in bed with the discriminators, the segregationists and the racists!

Barney says that he wants to build partnerships with the entire city. Biga may have misconstrued his words, but I don't think so – Barney probably got verbose and said so much that the editors had to cut some stuff out, hence the elipses. But he said enough: he wants to build partnerships with the entire city. Here's the question that this transplant from Iowa should ask: where, in the annals of history, have whites in Omaha sought to build any partnerships with North Omaha black people? I'm not talking about the tokens that they handpick, I'm talking about black people whose lives are in disarray? They haven't, so why do we always have to be the ones who want to build bridges and bridge gaps and all that? Because those doing it don't know what to do and they want to get paid. So they "go along to get along," as the saying goes.

Barney said that, "in evolving over time we've stayed true to our mission." That is an admission that everything that I have charged the Empowerment Network with is true. They have not stopped selling out North Omaha for a single minute; they have stayed true despite the fact that their anti-violence "programs" have failed, despite the fact that they haven't provided any housing, haven't created any meaningful, sustainable jobs, and certainly haven't change the physical plant of North Omaha. So they will remain the same; the "evolution" will only take place as the conditions change. But they won't change because they'll be too busy staying "true" to their mission. And that mission is to make sure that the relative positions of blacks and whites – the powerless and the powerful – does not change to any marked degree.

Then Barney foolishly tries to delve into management principles when he opines, "It has to be bottom-up and top-down for it to be anywhere close to being successful — individuals, families, leaders at all levels working together collaboratively."

There's that word, "collaboratively." And what he has just described has never taken place in the history of Omaha. The only time it comes close is when white people are threatened with major protests, race riots or some other form of confrontation. The Martin Luther King Jr. "kiss the other cheek" crap does not work on these people. The ministers are afraid and they claim to be tight with God. So where does that leave Barney and those negroes who are seeking to work from the bottom up and the top down? How asinine!

And with their philosophy (conciliation, accommodation, acquiescence) and origins (Salem Baptist Church) laid out, the foolhardiness just keeps on coming. Observe:

> The effort started focusing on seven core areas: jobs, business-economic development, education-youth development, voting, violence prevention, housing-neighborhoods-transportation and engagement. Evidence of the Network's wide reach was seen during its annual Harmony Week (May 21-29), when dozens of organizations and thousands of people across the Metro participated in expressions of unity and community engagement. In 2009 the organization opened an office in the historic Jewell Building in the heart of North O, across from the Omaha Star.

What effort? Earlier Biga wrote that Omaha's Empowerment Network targeted 13 areas for improvement," remember. Now it's seven areas that they are "focusing on." Focus is nothing unless it is followed up with a coherent plan on how to address what you're focusing on. And since they have no solutions they engage in foolishness and frolic as evidenced by its "annual Harmony Week." This is something that has always been used as a public relations campaign; have an event, give away free food, take photos and make sure the media is there. And because there are a lot of people in attendance, silly journalists like Biga can conclude that it is "evidence of the Network's wide reach."

But the preceding excerpt contains another key: the one that shows the interlocking directorates that exist in most "movements" that take place in Omaha. That is where the same people are working for different groups but make sure that the same goals and inactivity remain par for the course. It's similar to "six degrees of separation:" The Empowerment Network is housed across the street from the no-longer-relevant Omaha Star newspaper. It is in a building that is historical, but is also owned by the Omaha Economic Development Corporation, a shill for the city powers that be. And if OEDC is involved, that means that the city is not very far behind because that is who OEDC director Michael Maroney reports to and receives his piecemeal projects from.

So in addition to financial control by Suzie Buffett, we can now see that this so-called "coalition," this "network" is really nothing more than an adjunct to the city, just like NOCD was back in 1972 when it was formed. If you know your history, you won't fall prey to manipulated manifestations of it as in this case: the same old scams with different appearances and "players."

These people seem to think that marketing and public relations (remember Willie Barney's former job in Iowa) is the same thing as tangible production or community success. Read the following:

> The Network boosted its presence via an expanded website,
> Facebook page and Revive! Omaha Magazine, which Barney's
> SMB Enterprises LLC publishes. A TV spot features Network
> leaders reciting, like a creed, the Empowerment credo:
> "We can change Omaha. It's time to rebuild the village. Family
> by family, block by block, school by school, church by church,
> business by business. Each person doing their part. Working
> together, let's transform Omaha. Do your part. Live the
> covenant."

Websites and credos – all public relations. Talking about what they "can" do, but not doing it. Citing idealistic platitudes as if they were accomplishments. All this has been done, on a lesser technological level, of course, throughout the history of community development efforts in Omaha. Barney publishes a magazine and probably pays himself; he sells ads from which the revenue also probably goes into his pocket. Add to that the fact that he is on the payroll, and it is in his best interests to keep his mouth shut and, in exchange, the white man will let him wallow in his substanceless inactivity.

But there's more

> The Network's first full-time staffer was Quaites-Ferris, a former deputy assistant to former Mayor Mike Fahey said. Three-and-a-half years in, the Network has a track record. Barney said whatever course the Network adopts, it relies on others to carry it out. "At the end of the day it's ENCAP, the Urban League, Omaha Economic Development Corporation that are doing the work. But I think because we're here we've helped facilitate potentially more partnerships than would have happened before."

If it is indeed true that "three and a half years in, the Network as a track record," then produce it. List the accomplishments, not the intentions or plans. List how many families you've helped and jobs you've created. Three and a half years and you have a website and a credo.

Another connection is Quaites-Ferris, who worked for the Mayor of Omaha. All these connections and the people can't see that there is no way that the Empowerment Network could be independent? Barney can't cite examples of this "track record" they've got because anything that they do is going to have to have the blessing (read: permission) of the powers that be, the Omaha elites. And if he is bragging about "the work" that the Urban League, ENCAP (formerly Greater Omaha Community Action) and OEDC are doing, then he's citing three groups that have done even less than the Empowerment Network.

These are groups that have been around for decades, and have nothing to show for it but social work. They do nothing for the masses of people and can't get involved in any problems against the city because they, like the Network, are beholden to the city. OEDC gets CDBG money from the City of Omaha Planning Department, ENCAP survives off of Community Service Block Grants, and the Urban League is a site for the Nebraska Department of Social Services. None of them would dare bite the hand that feeds.

It's a lost cause. The Empowerment Network is the latest in a long string of "minority fronts" that the City of Omaha comes up with whenever they feel their federal status (grant money) may be threatened. And in the final analysis, its all about the money.

Barney boasts that the Network has, "helped facilitate potentially more partnerships than would have happened before." And that is their claim to fame: becoming partners with groups that have been here longer than they have and, as a result, should have been doing more.

Even the quasi-critics of the Network display an abysmal ignorance of the gravity of the situation, akin to those Native Americans that sold out their own people to the U.S. cavalry. For instance:

> Malcolm X Memorial Foundation president Sharif Liwaru said he feels the Network's facilitator rather than direct service provider role "is still hard for people to grasp."Barney concurred. While Liwaru and community activist Leo Louis feel the Network effectively engages established organizations and leaders, they advocate more outreach be done to new, more loosely organized groups as well as to youths. "We're doing more to really make sure it is an inclusive process," said Barney."If they don't come, we'll go to them, and we're not perfect, we make mistakes, but we keep pushing forward."

There is nothing "hard to grasp" about a group of people who pontificate, put signs on lawns claiming that "enough is enough" and then whenever you hear about them, they're having meetings, talking with the police, and socializing with some of the people who are a part of the on-going problem. Maybe Liwaru doesn't want to admit what he knows – but he's not stupid.

Biga calls someone named Leo Louis a "community activist." I always wanted to know how such a title is bestowed. I figured it out: white people use it has a warning label for people who are working for a group or cause they they (whites) don't agree with. I never met Louis and I wouldn't' t know him from Adam's house cat. He has no record to speak of, but just because this white reporter referred to him as a "community activist," he's already got my approval. Why? Because I'm sure that Louis didn't introduce himself as, "Hi – I'm a community activist." This is a label that white people reserve for those who have not bought into their program.

Barney claims that Network is doing all it can to make it "an inclusive process." Earlier he talked about bottoms-up and top-down strategy. But here is the clincher: that strategy was applied only to people who they (the Network) consider to be "worthy." If the process was inclusive, then the product would be inclusive and diverse. It is not; the Network consists of people who think they are leaders but the people they are supposed to be serving are left to social service agencies and the usual do-nothing groups like the Urban League, the NAACP and on an economic level, OEDC.

> In mid-2008 the Network noted workforce development gaps
> for at-risk youth and launched a life skills and jobs program. No
> one wanted a summer like 2007, when there were 31 reported
> shootings in 31 days during one stretch. Program participants
> included kids failing in school and drop-outs , ex and active
> gang members.

The first thing the Network should have noticed was the "workforce development gap," as they call it. When I met and talked with Dick Davis, he had it – unemployment – as a priority on his list. But now this group is doling out chump change short term jobs and trying to call it a victory. Every summer the government would provide funding for youth jobs. Then it started drying up but cities picked up some of the slack. What the Network is doing is nothing new and it's nothing profound. It's a fearful response to the gun violence and this proves what I said earlier: if you want to get the white man's attention, you have to use violence or the threat of it. That' all he knows.

As for the kids failing in school, Ben Gray is a part of the Network. He's supposed to be the director of the African-American Achievement Team – although he dropped out of college himself. There was no progress and, in fact, on his watch, the test scores for black kids have gotten worse. Aren't any of these guys accountable to truly act in a way that leads to "empowerment" and not pacification or placation?

Here was their strategy:

> Barney and Gray contacted employers to secure 150 paid
> internships. The program was repeated last summer, with
> enrollees split between returning and new participants. Barney
> said many "transitioned back into school, some went on to get
> GEDs and others got offers for fulltime work." 2009 saw
> hundreds more jobs created by federal stimulus funds and
> private donors. The Urban League facilitated.

Internships? Assuming that Biga is using the terminology that he got directly from Gray and Barney, this approach to jobs is, at best piecemeal and at most, elitist. An internship, by definition, is *"any official or formal programs to provide practical experience for beginners in an occupation or profession," or a position as a participant in such programs. "* This is what college students do to gain experience; these young kids need full-time, permanent jobs, not a chance to get a whiff of what it's like to get a check and then, in a few weeks the experience is over! Where is the community on this "internship" approach to jobs for young people? Internships, but the very name, have a time limit!

Then Barney says that they "transitioned back into school." This goes to the heart of what I said: internships are for students and those who plan to go to school. This is an elitist program when you consider the fact that most of those youth don't want to go to school, have been pushed out or have dropped out. Where is the city's contribution? Where is the spending of the CDBG and CSBG monies? Why should these people be waiting for stimulus funds? And these private donors are rich – why doesn't Buffett contribute some of his billions to a long-term job effort? Why do black kids always have to be guinea pigs so that megalomaniacs and pseudo-leaders can make the white man think that they're "on the job"?

Then Biga and the Network, undoubtedly working in tandem, flip the script:

> Minus any federal funds in 2010, the number of summer jobs provided at-risk youth this year will be closer to 500, rather than last year's 800. "In a lot of instances we basically have to start from scratch — we have to teach people how to fill out an application, how to successfully interview, how to do some things we take for granted," said Gray. "This is a big job because you've got to change attitudes as well as change behavior. Neither is easy, but you've got to get it done because the only other choice is to build more jails and at the end of the day that's costing us three to four times as much money as to provide jobs and job training and proper schooling."

There was supposed to be a plan. The largest church in the city was where Barney laid it out. Gray is on the city council and has access to funds. He carries water for a Mayor who has access to a contingency fund. What is all this about going back to the basics or starting from scratch? This is re-inventing the wheel: programs, assuming black people are stupid, take them back to how to fill out an application, how to successfully interview. According to Gray, these are things that "we take for granted."

How could he take it for granted? He had one job for over twenty years carrying a camera. Before that he enlisted in the military. Where is his experience filling out an application? The problem is always the black community, a community that worked harder than anyone else when there was work. No one works harder than black women, for starters. Gray doesn't have confidence in his own people, which is why he paints a picture of (1) acceptance of the piecemeal programs offered or (2) risk being locked up.

His appeal is to the system because that is who builds the jails. He's looking at black employment as a "savings" approach to community development – the market approach. At no time does Gray use the history of neglect and abuse by the system to get it to do the right thing.

Clearly, these men are not economists or job creators and, in fact, they are poor planners. More evidence follows:

> Barney said the group launched a multifaceted violence prevention collaboration. "It's not just telling folks, 'Don't do this,' now we're providing options." Impact One Community Connection, formerly New World Youth Development, was formed to do gang intervention-prevention. The Network also collaborates with ENCAP, the Eastern Nebraska Community Action Partnership (formerly GOACA).

Earlier I offered insights about the importance of nominality – that is, naming something. From your child to an organization, a name is the first thing that anyone comes into contact with, plain and simple.

So they've changed their name from New World Youth Development – grandiose and untrue, to Impact One Community Connection, a definite downsizing in scope and of course, so generic that it means all things to all people. Impact One? What the hell does that mean?

The Network "collaborates" (there's that word again) with ENCAP, which is formerly GOCA (not "GOACA" as Biga writes). So what? ENCAP is a social service agency that provides mental health counseling, free groceries and rental assistance. Over the years what else has it done. It's always had leadership that was more likely to take a few days off and meet some woman in the park than planning for North Omaha. From Charles Lane to Dr. Ben Ebong to Karen Shepherd to whomever is running it now. GOCA is a social service approach to community development, not a social engineer.

People with a limited track record in their commitment to the major issues impacting North Omaha (police brutality, utilities assistance, racist evictions and other housing discrimination issues, mis-education of kids in the Omaha Public Schools, etc.) continue to attract Biga in his painting of a portrait of profundity:

> Teresa Hunter said she, Barney and others were impressed "a group of youths wanted to continue meeting and talking about the issues and the remedies. They wanted to keep coming back and to make a change." In turn, said Barney, participants "were amazed somebody cared enough to spend all that time one-on-one with them and to help them get a job. They will flat out tell you no one has ever given them these opportunities before. Even some of the kids on the street that everybody totally discounts and that people said there's no way you're going to reach, well, we reached them."

Who cares if these people are "impressed" with kids wanting to talk about issues? Had they approached them earlier they would have known it long ago. Had they not assumed that young people "didn't care," they would have learned it long ago. Had they been involved in the community's concerns, they would have known that. These people are afraid of black kids, and that's the problem. Whatever the white man says about these kids, these negroes believe it. And the only time that they're "impressed" is when the kids come out to one of THEIR programs where they have those kids sign in and then they can run to the white man and say, "See boss – we had good attendance." Either that or turn the sheet over to the police for review. I wouldn't put anything past people like these, who admittedly work so closely with those who have only done harm to North Omaha.

Barney claims that kids told him that no one has ever given them these opportunities before. That is a lie. To begin with, opportunities has never been in short supply: black people get "opportunities" all the time. But the issue is what is the source of this "opportunity" and where is it going to lead you? Going to a meeting and learning how to conduct yourself in a job interview is an "opportunity," but without a guaranteed job, it's nothing more than an exercise in futility.

The Empowerment Network has the opportunity to do right by North Omaha, but the proof is in the pudding: as long as they don't make decisions on their own, as long as they cater and kowtow to whites with power (while they have none), the opportunity is going to have the same conclusion as many opportunities that are provided to you by an outsider: *non-productive*.

If you close your eyes and talk to Barney, Hunter, Gray and the other self-appointed leaders, you wouldn't be able to distinguish between what they say or what some white suburbanite has to say. There is nothing culturally inclusive about their plan or their attitudes. Using the deficit model, they assume the worst about North Omaha and view themselves as "missionaries" who are hell-bent on "helping out those savages." The same tactics that white folks, using the social work approach, have historically approached North Omaha.

Continuing:

> Recruiting them, he said, was largely the work of the late Roy Davenport and of Gray. Both brought longtime gang intervention experience. The Network's aligned itself with the Omaha Police Department, particularly the Northeast Precinct, and North Omaha Weed & Seed to do Safe Night Outs and other efforts for improving police-community relations. Gray, who leads an emergency response team, said street work is where it's at in reaching past or present gangbangers.

The late Roy Davenport and his "Ambassadors program" was actually something I advised him with. He didn't even have a name for it and I came up with "ambassadors." Then I never saw him again because somehow, he got hooked up with Ben Gray. What Biga doesn't mention while he drops names and pretends like he knows the history, Davenport got into some trouble of a sexual orientation nature and was afraid that the other person was going to go public; so Davenport killed himself. Everything and everyone that Ben Gray associates himself with seems to take a nose-dive based on that relationship.

Next, they admit that they work with the police. When Triple One worked with police they were black and they cared about and lived in the community: Danny Hayes, Tariq Al-Amin, Marvin McClarty and so on. These guys are working with white cops and the Northeast Precinct is not the most progressive place in the world. If Weed and Seed is involved, then there's grant money somewhere down the road. "Safe Night Outs" is a national program and the Network needs to stop taking credit for it.

Now Biga's own words and beliefs mix with Ben Gray's as he writes, "Gray, who leads an emergency response team, said street work is where it's at in reaching past or present gangbangers." This is supposed to be a news article or a feature – who used the term "gangbangers"? This is what pisses these kids off: they are labeled and black people accept those labels. If Gray said it, he should be ashamed of himself as an elected official; if Biga came up with it based on what Gray said, then they should both be ashamed. But weak minds think alike, and this is but one example.

Look at how Gray re-invents the wheel and describes and takes credit for the actions of what many others have done long before he was on the scene:

> "You got to meet them where they are. If you are not willing to
> get out in those blocks, in those neighborhoods, in those houses
> where they live, you are not going to reach those young people.
> You gotta be at the hospitals, you gotta be at the funerals, you
> gotta be constantly talking about not retaliating … about going
> in a different direction. That's very time consuming, painstaking,
> difficult work and there are no set hours. We have ex-gang
> members employed through Impact One. They monitor the
> streets on a regular basis."

When did Ben Gray ever "get out there" in the neighborhood other than to campaign for office (and it's doubtful that he even did it then)? Ben Gray knows there are people out there who don't like him because he's known as someone who will do anything for a buck and that he's linked to Suzie Buffett, a white woman who calls the shots for the black community's main politicos (Brenda Council,

Chris Rodgers, Ben Gray). If he went door to door he wouldn't be able to control the response because he'd be on someone else's property. If Ben Gray is nothing else, he is a control freak, but he only seeks it when he's got the upper hand (a microphone in his hand, the city council seat, etc.) He's outlining a strategy that any community organizer would undertake – that doesn't mean that he did it.

Take note of where he thinks the young people are: hospitals and funerals. That's after the fact contact, in my book. If you go to their houses, then what are you saying to them? Gray never personalized the process or the strategy. He says "YOU" gotta do this – that doesn't mean he did it or has the guts to do it. Maybe those "ex-gang members" (in reality, there is no such thing – "blood in, blood out") are the ones he uses to go door-to-door because he claims they "monitor the streets on a regular basis." Are they paid or are they acting as volunteers?

Since he thinks he's a leader, he feels that his kudos and approval means something. Check it out:

> Gray lauds the Network for "putting its neck on the line" to even do this outreach, saying it's a microcosm for how a wounded community can heal. "We have people that have been disappointed so much they're not willing to necessarily buy-in until they have seen some stability in you going down the road getting a few things accomplished, and then you'll hopefully get that groundswell of people that will come on board with you."

Which members of the Network are putting their necks on the line? Is he implying that all of them do? Is he? If you are doing outreach, why would you be putting your neck on the line if you have credibility? Is he saying that young kids are "dangerous"?

Then comes the closest thing to a confession of inadequacy that you'll ever hear from Ben Gray. It's where he says, *"We have people that have been disappointed so much they're not willing to necessarily buy-in until they have seen some stability in you going down the road getting a few things accomplished, and then you'll hopefully get that groundswell of people that will come on board with you."*

It's because of people like him, getting caught time and time again in things that are later swept under the rug. Impregnating an intern at KETV not once, but twice. She's still in Omaha but doesn't want to bring attention to the fact that she sued KETV and finally won – he helped her do it. Why isn't this public? What about the consecutive lies that he told about taking over as publisher of the Omaha Crusader, lies that served as stall tactics more than anything else? And where is that big time attorney that he was supposed to bring in to defend black police officer Tariq Al-Amin when the police department was trying to fire him for statements they say he made (actually, it was me) on a cable television program?

Where was the response to Senator Chambers' *Omaha Star* essay about how he (Gray) lied about having met with and interacted with Malcolm X? What about his flip-flop on a vote that bought CVS Pharmacy to an area of the city that was outside of his district? Why the 24 change of mind? Bribe, perhaps?

People talk, and this is the talk on the streets. It reached me all the way in Dallas so if that is the case, then the streets of North Omaha must be permeated with these kinds of allegations. Some of them I know of personally, so there can be no doubt that when Gray talks about people being "disappointed," he is a part of the reason for that. The Jews give him an award and he literally disappears from involvement in community coverage while serving as host of "Kaleidoscope."

I don't know Barney, *but you judge a man by his words and his works*. If his words are any indicator, then he is yet another in a long line of "sunshine soldiers" who march out to "save North Omaha" and then end up working for and with the city administration. Take note of the following general truisms and vanilla philosophy with no mention of race, discrimination or any of the things that are at the base of the problems he claims to be combatting:

> Barney said the Network "has the opportunity to really make a tremendous difference. Some of it will be over time, some of it will be dramatic," such as the 36 percent reduction in gun violence in July-August 2008. Barney said he's sure some people feel the Network effort is not open enough, or that they don't have a voice. He wants them to contact him. "We'll sit down and we'll meet and we'll listen and try the best we can to make adjustments." "We are building a long-term foundation. We're getting more and more people engaged, more people are stepping forward. That doesn't mean the violence is going to stop today or next week. I keep saying to folks, 'It did not happen overnight and it will not be solved overnight. 'We've seen some things slowly move in the right direction."

The Network has "the opportunity," he says, "to really make a tremendous difference" and "some of it will be over time, some of it will be dramatic." Every single person in Omaha has the opportunity to make a tremendous difference, but very few *seize upon* or *take* those opportunities. That's essentially the difference between leaders and followers.

Additionally, with "over time" and "dramatic" are not opposites – something can be done over time or in the short term and still be dramatic. This is what happens when people who can't think on their feet get interviewed and when the person doing the interview is editing their words. The Network has had more than ample opportunity, but an organization without a sense of direction is like a rat on a treadmill: movin' but not going anyplace!

You cannot take a two month reduction in anything and consider it a trend or a success. There are a plethora of variables that would go into a reduction of gun violence, including the fact that those acts of violence were instigated by the police and as such, the perpetrators are locked up; the fact that the police upgraded their patrols; the fact that in response to these shootings, the people in the area became more aware and more careful about where they were going. This alleged "decline" in gun violence cannot be laid at the door of the Empowerment Network and anyone who thinks that is an idiot.

If he's sure about something, why not act on it. If you are being accused of not being open enough, then change it. Why should people have to contact you to do something that you claim to already know? When my constituents said that I was too forceful at meetings and intimidated them, I stopped going to meetings and handed the agenda, the plans and the gavel over to Robert Bauldwin. That is what leaders do: they make decisions and they realize that the organization and the effort are more important than their presence. If they are real leaders, their presence will linger on even when they are not physically there.

Even if people do contact him, he offers them nothing in the way of a guarantee – he doesn't assure them that the problem will be fixed. Instead, what does he say? *"We'll sit down and we'll meet and we'll listen and try the best we can to make adjustments."* Try as best we can? Perhaps, in the final analysis, this is all that the Network will ever end up doing – especially once the money dries up and they are left only with the depth of their commitments and convictions.

As if the flimsy explanations and jejune excuses were not enough, now comes more "explanations" from Barney:

> Barney said he's sure some people feel the Network effort is not open enough, or that they don't have a voice. He wants them to contact him. "We are building a long-term foundation. We're getting more and more people engaged, more people are stepping forward. That doesn't mean the violence is going to stop today or next week. I keep saying to folks, 'It did not happen overnight and it will not be solved overnight. 'We've seen some things slowly move in the right direction."

It should be clear after reading my analysis that the Empowerment Network leadership doesn't have a clue. The man who was the brains behind it, Dick Davis, drew up diagrams, charts and had models that I personally saw. I don't know if he turned it over to the wrong people or what, but this is not what I saw when I was in his office working to develop long term strategies. And for the record, I was the one who bought the concept of "empowerment" to North Omaha; it was only after I left for Dallas and my assistant, a senior brother named Henry Mason died, that the conferences stopped being held and the empowerment concept was put on hold.

The article (mercifully) concludes:

> Geraldine Wesley with Long School Neighborhood Association embraces the Network "getting people's hopes up to empower" North O, adding, "If they carry out all the things they intend to do, it would be good." "Well, right now its just ideas, there's nothing concrete as far as I know," she said. I am waiting for the results. It's going to be a long process, I know that. I hope I'll live to see it."

Hope. Dreams. Wishing. Have faith. Keep on believing. I sicken of these types of platitudes as our community suffers, not on only a daily basis, but on what seems to be an hourly basis. There are people who are ill and can't get around, there are people who are hungry and who are wondering how they are going to feed their children, there are people whose utilities have been shut off, there are people whose cars sit in the driveway because they can't even afford a gallon of gas. And then you have people prancing around the community talking about "empowerment" and they can't even help pay one light bill?

That was one of the knocks against the Black Panther Party back in the day. They would talk all this stuff about revolution, but the question would come back from some other group or individual, "how can you talk about revolution and you can't even take out one police station?" The Panthers, to their credit, did create and pioneer the feeding of kids in day care and they did other good work as well. But this Empowerment Network is not feeding anybody, and no one's life is being improved because of the Network's presence. They take on no issues, they don't advocate and they won't lobby.

These have been my views of the Empowerment Network. I'll put my 25-plus years of experience and community development up against anyone in that Network any day of the week. It should be clear who would be victorious.

<u>Understand the Politics of Race and Reality: The
1997 Race Commission Study</u>

As you can see in the previous section, much of the black leadership doesn't have a clue; like birdies in a nest waiting for the mama bird to drop a worm in their collective mouths, these black "men" are nothing more than comic relief for the powers that be. No one who knows anything about community or neighborhood development could possibly be taking them seriously. Read their words again: if they had even a scintilla of dignity, they would retract those words and leave intelligent statements to people who know what they're talking about. But they are not alone.

I selected the following report and analysis (only the "Introduction" section has been analyzed in this paper) to demonstrate that naivete (ignorance) about race relations even impacts on those who are supposed to be major decision makers. The conclusions of the race commission's report have long been forgotten but that was because they were "forgettable" the minute the ink dried: no concrete ideas, grandiose and irrelevant quotes and a plethora of conceptual mistakes that I was more than happy to point out in the analysis that follows.

You have to understand your own direction and vision and as importantly, understand the role that "race" has played in the development of Omaha. If you can do these two things, you will be miles ahead of the men and women who were interviewed in the previous section.

Following is my analysis of the introduction section of the 1997 "race commission" study that was conducted by the Omaha city administration and a team of more than 100 people, handpicked by then mayor Hal Daub.

The 1997 Race Commission Study and Its Introductory Comments: Retrospective Critique and Commentary

In January of 2000 when the city issues a study which claimed that race relations were never better, I was angered by such a false conclusion. At that point I issued a "counter-document," in rebuttal to a "report" that was subsequently issued.

The method was not a new one. In fact, it represented what now, in retrospect, appears to be an historical tendency, documented in a work written in 1971 called, *Odyssey: Journal Through Black America.* In one segment, long-time Omaha dentist Earle Person had this observation:

> "When the whites put together their new downtown area, their slogan was: "Can do." We [blacks in Omaha] saw that the slogan for the Near North Side was: "Won't do." The prime movers just say, "Well, we'll try a few little things, form a committee, call in an outside research organization, make a study." And they do survey after survey after survey, and all of them get stuck away in some file..." (Selby & Selby, 1971: 290)

How prescient Person was!

North Omahans – the most oft-studied group in the history of the city and, as a result, we remain the poorest. Why? Because if we empower ourselves, there will be no one else left for them to study; no one else for them to exploit; no one else for them to document as being poor, and then taking that information and sending it to Washington, D.C. in exchange for Federal grant monies!

The city's philosophy, based upon the research of their spending patterns, appears to be clear: if they are going to do anything to help North Omaha residents, it will *only be if there are Federal grant dollars available*. Even in this "race report," as you will see, the employment section tells the reader that the key is the "economic development section" of the report. And when you turn to that section, all you see being discussed are Enterprise Zones – a federal program! The message: if blacks want jobs, then they had better pray that Enterprise Zones works! Meanwhile, local employers will continue to discriminate, refuse to hire, arbitrarily fire and otherwise neglect any blacks who apply for jobs in the conventional manner.

Generally speaking, the "Report" by the so-called Commission would receive a grade of "D-minus" if it were handed into me in a college-level course. Take note of what these white people and their "colored quislings" have done. They begin with a report on race and divide it into sections. But alas, each subcommittee digs in only to find none of them knows anything about race relations and indeed, that they are themselves at least partially responsible for its existence. So what do they do? Each section degenerates into a "how to guide"! And that is what you can expect if you read a copy of it: a dialogue on how each of the areas – health care, housing, education, employment, economic development and media – can improve its training, its outlook, its promotional materials, its examinations, its recruiting and so on. Very little in terms of concrete ideas about how each of these areas has harmed North Omaha.

The fact of the matter is, there can be no serious social change if the players who prevent such change are in charge. This is a common sense reality that the "leadership" of Omaha appear to be too ignorant to understand. As I've written elsewhere,

> Black Omahans , with few exceptions, have very low self-esteem and apparently do not care what takes place in their community. Whites have traditionally known this, and they knew it as far back as 1977. The Urban League quotes "one city official who has boasted that 'Omaha today is host to one of the neater, more law-abiding black ghettos in the country." (Urban League of Nebraska, 1978: 7) And in a 1977 survey by WOWT, it was found that race relations, as a perceived problem, ranked tenth behind such areas of

preoccupation as recreation, transportation and city sewers.
(Stelly, 1998: p. 12)

The Commission was an inept, cowardly group of people who didn't attend most of the meetings. Dr. Everett Reynolds of the Omaha NAACP documented the poor attendance at many of the meetings, and the black community knows that this is just another, in a long line, of attempts to make it appear as if Omaha is changing for the better and that race relations are improving when, in reality, nothing could be further from the truth.

On the cover of the document is a quote by of all people, Robert F. Kennedy Jr. A savior to many, Kennedy's track record with blacks is questionable when you remember the role he played in the arrest of Dr. Martin Luther King Jr., and his incessant attempts to try to get civil rights advocates to "slow down."

No Kennedy had any love for black people. And, like far too many white people, he was a racist. But these white people view him as a liberal and a progressive. So the question is, why would Hal Daub, a conservative Republican who is also a racist, have a quote from Robert F. Kennedy on the cover of this report? Why would Hal Daub have a picture of the hands of black and brown and white kids joined together when, in reality, he has hurt the families of brown, black and red people ever since he took office?

With such hypocrisy evident on the cover of the report, you can imagine the depth of contradictions that lie within the covers. Following is documentation and discussion of the foolishness, shallowness and perfidious contents of the *Omaha Commission on Community and Race Relations Reports and Recommendations, December, 1999.*

The Name of The Organization

While claiming that there was no governmental influence or input into the document, the very fact that they call themselves a commission puts the lie to such claims. A "Commission" is defined as "a group of people given official authorization to perform certain functions or duties." Furthermore, in her section of the report, Director of Job Training Diane Thomas puts her report in memo form, addressed to guess who? Mayor Hal Daub.

None of the people on the Commission understand the gravity of the race problem in Omaha. But they do, however, have one thing in common: they all benefit from it. From Eddie Staton, who will do anything to remain on the government dole and Danye Etchinaw, a woman who belongs to the money-grubbing organization which calls itself La Belle Afrique, to Carrie Murphy who works at the racist KMTV-Channel 3 and Rita Melgares, queen of the conservative

Latinos, they are all Daub supporters on some level, or they are the minions of people who ARE Daub supporters.

And this explains why the report amounts to nothing even resembling a relevant report. That is why they call the group who wrote it the Commission on Community and Race Relations. Had they left out the community, the lack of experience and knowledge on race issues would have been even MORE obvious; by adding the "community" dimension, those who miss the boat – meaning most of them – can claim that they were speaking "generically" or "didn't see race as a concern."

Kellie Paris-Asaka, the director of the Human Relations Department, appeared on Channel 7's "Kaleidoscope" on January 9, 2000. She was concerned about the criticisms of the report and made some statements which showed that, indeed, there is an ulterior motive to the recommendations put forth in the Commission's report.

For instance, she expressed disappointment that the City Council did not allocate her the $40,000 she needed for a "race survey." But she claims that she still wants the money and, if the Commission no longer wants a survey, she hopes "we can use the money to effectuate the recommendations of the Commission." Well, before her appearance, nowhere in the document does the city, the county or anyone else devote or commit money to any of the "recommendations" in the Report. On the contrary, one of my major criticisms is that what few good recommendations there are appear to be part of things already taking place. No money then, was committed.

One thing about her appearance was that she admitted that this was the best that she and her cohorts could do. In her words, "I put a lot of work into getting this report published … it was a powerful recommendation … this was a sincere effort to start a dialogue on race relations in Omaha."

Back in 1995 when I went on the air on Channel 22, I vowed to the community that it was my goal to take the issue of racism out of the bar and the interracial bedroom and to raise it to the level of social debate. Ernie's show came along and did the same thing. Programs like "Black Male Roundtable,""The Khalil Ben Ashanti Hour of Power,""Protecting the Village," and "Show of Truth" did the same thing. The Triple One Neighborhood Association and the Parent's Union, both created by me, did the same thing in the areas of community development and education, respectively.

How then, can Ms. Paris believe or open her distended mouth to say that this poorly written document and its pretentious authors have "started a dialogue on race relations" or anything else, for that matter? When I was addressing the race issue on my show, it was people like Paris and her cronies who were cowering at home gasping for air and acting shocked and amazed. Like her boss, Mayor Hal Daub, she is a hypocrite.

She told "Kaleidoscope" host Ben Gray that it was the findings of the Commission that "race played a significant role in" the particular problems that the Commission addressed and finally, that "race is an issue." Where has this silly woman been for the past decade? She handled the Crossroads Mall case back in 1995, after I brought the parties together and exposed the racism in the case. *And she was so inept, she had a fling with one of the plaintiffs and ended up losing the case, anyway!* This is the kind of track record that the woman who now heads the Human Relations Department brings with her. And if she couldn't handle an easy, slam dunk case like *Kemp, Kemp and Colthirst vs. Crossroads Mall and Simon Management*, then who is she to make it appear as if she knows anything about race, racism or race relations? Like her boss, she's a jack of *few* trades and a master of one: tommin'!

She claimed that the survey was "a tool to measure progress." Here's how you measure progress in race relations: look at the segregation of Omaha today and compare it with segregation of 10 years ago. Is there any change? No. Are more blacks being hired? No. Has the relative income between whites and blacks narrowed? No. If there was no racism, would there be any need for her department? No. And finally, if there was no racism, why did her own boss, Hal Daub, attempt to do away with the Department as recently as three years ago?

So it's clear what's on his mind: if he can't destroy it because of black community support, he'll put someone in charge of it who will run it into the ground. Enter: Kellie Paris Asaka! Her ignorance of racism shows when Ben Gray asked her why they didn't use the discrimination data from the files of the Human Relations Department or the Nebraska Equal Opportunity Commission. She said that while they had information in the areas of employment and housing, there wasn't enough data in the areas of health care, media, education and so on. After all, she explained, "we determined that racism could go beyond the traditional areas."

Oh, really? Paris is an attorney. The "traditional areas" of discrimination are the ones which paved the way for the others! She knows that housing and employment discrimination were both sanctioned by the system as recently as 1950! She has to know something about the racist mindset because that is what discrimination is: it is the action based on a racist attitude. Now since that is the case, if you find it in an area like employment, that paves the way for the exercise of racism in other spheres: where you can afford to live, how your children fare in school, the quality of health care you receive, where you can go socially and so on. If this woman doesn't know this, then she is an insult to the Nebraska Bar, the

North Omaha community and anyone who is sincerely committed to learning about now to improve race relations in Omaha.

To paraphrase an age old adage, you judge a Commission by the reports it bears. And in this case, it is clear that the Commission created by Hal Daub and monitored by Hal Daub reflects the same naivete, racism and backwardness which Hal Daub exhibits every time he opens his mouth. This kind of ineptitude is evident in his cronies, from Mike Saklar and Brinker Harding, to Jim Cleary and now, Kellie Paris-Anaka.

As stated, this document is an exercise in futility, and starts off with what I view as "grandiose quotes" by the League of Cities.

The first such quote, from the 1991 League of Cities document, titled, "Diversity and Governance," reads as follows: "The first requirement of city leaders is that they embrace diversity and affirm equal rights for all. From that there can be no retreat." This is not true. City leaders need to ACT on that which has already been confirmed by law and by God. Their affirmation is unnecessary if they would but just act.

On the same page is another quote, this one from "Building a Nation of Communities," also by the League of Cities: "Deep-seated problems such as racism, economic exclusion, and a sense of political powerlessness often stand in the way of residents feeling they have a equal stake in their communities' success."

"Often stand in the way"? Are there times when racism, economic exclusion and a sense of political powerlessness WORK for people of color, or anyone else, for that matter? This statement, by being quoted, is a case of the blind leading the blind. This proves that what white people (and their Negro lackies) find relevant, black people feel the opposite about.

To ensure balance, no doubt, there are two more quotes from the League of cities, the 1999 Futures Report. The question at the top of the page asks, "How Can We Undo Racism?" The first answer is "By Changing Ourselves," and the explanation reads,

> On the one hand, working against racism means changing what we, as
> individuals and elected leaders, are doing to keep racism alive – for
> example, by separating ourselves, intentionally or not, from individuals
> of different races, or by not speaking up when those around us make
> racist comments.

The question is, why haven't white folks done it? The answer is, because they cannot. As Dr. Frances Welsing teaches, racism is a matter of genetic survival for those people. If they fraternize and have sex, the product is a child of color. For their own survival on this planet, they must shield themselves from the brown gene, which is both sociogenically and genetically more powerful than the "white" gene.

The second answer is, "By Changing our Policies and Institutions," and the quote says:

> Dismantling racism also means changing the policies and the social and institutional systems that allow racism to remain an oppressive force – for example, by enabling police to stop motorists because of the color of their skin or by permitting banks to treat loan applicants of different races differently.

The policies and institutions are aimed at maintaining the white supremacy structure which protects them genetically. Segregation is one way that they maintain social separation. One need only read "The Cress Theory of Color Confrontation and Racism" or *The Isis Papers: The Keys to the Colors* to better understand why white people act so foolishly when they must confront their neighbors of color.

The selection of these quotes shows that Commission members are out of tune with the racial reality of the times. Even the "Negroes" who were members of the Commission, had they cared anything about their white colleagues, would not have allowed these dunderhead quotes to be used. But it appears that neither side really cares about the other and the key was to hurriedly construct a document that the Mayor could use as evidence that he "cares about the negro people."

Well he failed and they failed. Following is evidence of these collective failures and reasons why the Report by the Commission on Community and Race Relations should be read carefully.

And then burned.

Next is the "Executive Summary."

The writers of the report were so limited in their research skills that they attempted to masquerade their shortcomings with irrelevant quotations, outmoded data and generic conclusions. An example lies in the following passage:

> Since the spring of 1998, volunteers from across this city have been actively engaged in research, analysis and assessment of race relations in Omaha, Nebraska … Racism in all its manifestations is an emotional topic for many, and is extremely difficult to talk about. Members of the committees experienced this as they strived to create actionable recommendations organizations, government and even individuals can embrace and implement. (p. 3)

More than half a year of research by all of these people, and their findings are as relevant as a term paper written by a third grader. The topic is only "emotional" to those who have practiced and benefited from it; blacks, Latinos and American Indians have been dealing with racism for so long, there is nothing to get emotional about. So the statement about emotion shows you which group constituted the majority – white folks. And that is why they "strived to create actionable recommendations" and didn't really create any. They tried to do all they could, but failed. They attempted to find solutions but didn't know how to define the problem, where to look for solutions, or how to analyze what they came across.

Furthermore, what are the academic credentials of these "volunteers"? What makes them think that they can conduct research? Not only that, but the report claims that these people were "actively engaged in research, analysis and assessment of the state of race relations in Omaha, Nebraska." If these people were so smart, they would have already found a "solution." The fact that they are, as a collective, intellectually inadequate can be seen in the difficulty that this town has in luring and keeping major businesses; when all is said and done, the State of Nebraska and Omaha lose out to such hinterland capitals as Alabama and Utah!

But this raises an important point: these people, both subconsciously and consciously, have such a low regard for race relations and improving race relations, that they feel that any layman, any clown off the corner can conduct "research." If we were studying the way to make relations better between white men and women, do you think the League of Women Voters or the Omaha chapter of the National Organization of Women would allow just "anybody" to conduct research in their behalf? No.

Only when it comes to the blacks and the Latinos do these arrogant white people think that they – the source of the problems we face – can also provide the solutions. They want to conduct research and do analysis on data when the problem stares them in the mirror every day; when they are sleeping with the problem; when they are employed by and do the bidding of the problem. This dishonesty is the basis of the report which explains why honest people must reject its contents, root and branch.

The poorly written and shabbily presented "reports" were explained, as follows:

> The reports in this package appear just as members of the
> subcommittees have submitted them. This is the information that these
> volunteers have compiled in each individual committee, on their own
> time over the last twenty months, without influence or input from any
> political factions in the City. (p. 3)

Almost two years of preparation, we now learn. And they want us to believe that during this period, the people who didn't know what they were doing didn't seek any assistance from anyone who works with the city, the university or anyone with expertise that they lacked? This is an absurd lie. The people involved had been benefiting from racism all their lives and most of them live in segregated neighborhoods. When confronted with having to challenge that which has become a way of life, it is no wonder they were left dumbfounded and why, after twenty months, the best they could come up with was 62 pages of dunce-like drivel.

To further the like, a "nonpolitical disclaimer" of sorts was provided by these intellectual midgets in the following passage:

> Subcommittees recruited members who were interested in making positive impact in the race relations arena. Political affiliation was a non-issue as subcommittees met each week or month to hammer out the essentials for improving race relations in our city. They sought out individuals who freely gave of their time and resources to look at Omaha race relations issues from a 360 degree viewpoint with the intent of finding facts, causes and solutions – not placing blame … (p. 3)

First of all, these people found no solutions. They simply regurgitated some general truisms that most people already knew. This, again, is attributable to their backwardness and dishonesty. Furthermore, they talk of not "placing blame;" it is not a matter of "blaming" anyone. It is a matter of "attributing responsibility," and we know on whose shoulders segregation, redlining, steering, consumer fraud, pilfering of Federal grant money, mis-education, and police harassment should be placed. It is not a matter of "blame," but a matter of those who practice these things to own up to them and realize that since they are so intertwined with the problem, they cannot possibly be a part of any solution.

If the subcommittee recruited members "who were interested in making positive impact in the race relations arena," why did they not share with the readers of the Report how they went about making those selections? How was the recruitment mechanism set up? Was it by word of mouth? Or was it by picking people who shared the same views and values? And since it most likely was the latter, how can one expect change when what we have on this subcommittee is really nothing more than the blind leading the blind?

How do you look at something with a "360 degree viewpoint?" What is a 360 degree viewpoint? How would you know if someone had the capacity to look at something with this kind of viewpoint? How did those doing the recruiting know who had or who did not have this viewpoint? If the subcommittee knows who has this view point and who does not, then does that mean that the committee can tell who is racist and who is not? The thoughts are flawed because the words used to describe the process are flawed. That is why nothing that comes from such divided approaches and mixed up ideas will work. As Karenga writes, "to divide the process is to deform the product."

The lies continue to mount, as the need to cover up the shabby work increases. Take note of the following attempt at an explanation:

> Cross sections of people from across the metropolitan area participated
> in the Omaha Commission on Race and Community Relations.
> Individuals from all walks of life were actively involved in all
> subcommittees. This means that leaders from community organizations,
> private and public sectors as well as front line concerned individuals
> were actively engage in the work of the commission. (p. 3)

This is a lie. Ultimately however, what they really mean is that everyone involved was selected, picked or recruited by someone else. And this means that what you ultimately had was a "clique of the unconscious," a coterie of kooks, a circle of pseudo-intellectuals. By banding together, they make it appear as if the issue of race is so complex and that they do not know what the problem is. The more people they recruited, the bigger the problem became because when it comes to race relations in Omaha, white people are the major problem, and their handpicked flunkies of color make solving the problem even more difficult.

In addition to the pervasive stupidity and racism that permeated the subcommittee, paternalism was also present. That is the only way to explain the cultural arrogance that lies behind the following statement:

> People of Color were able to openly discuss how they were affected in
> the seven focus areas … The impact of those leaders' participation is
> evident in the community partnerships that have been formed, and
> small, yet important change that have happened as a result of those
> forums. (p. 4)

How would white people know if people of color were "able to openly discuss how they were affected"? If these people of color felt some comfortable, then why even bother discussing racism, why not leave everything the way it is now? After all, they are sitting in the midst of racists and they are comfortable enough to say how they feel. This means that "equality" existed in that situation? Where then, is the equality and the "open ear" of the white man in the society at large? Nowhere to be found. And the reason it can't be found is the same reason why it didn't exist at these "playtime sessions" sponsored by the subcommittee: because both sides are being fake, with white people feigning liberalism and black people fooling those whites by "tomming." No sane solution can come out of a situation when the two parties involved are behaving in such a duplicitous and perfidious manner.

The preceding statement claims that the impact of "those leaders" participation can be seen in the community partnerships that have been formed. As a grant writer, I know that the buzzword of the 1990s was "partnership," just as the buzzword of the new century is "collaboration." At any rate, the only partnerships that are formed revolve around going after grant money and then splitting it; the white groups need the minority input for ideas and to meet Federal guidelines, and the blacks need the white resources and clout. This is not a "partnership" – it's an alienated arrangement.

Knowing that they were woefully inadequate, a day late and a dollar short, the charlatans who made up this subcommittee began applying qualifiers to their already shortsighted efforts. At one point they write,

> **… The original purpose of the commission was to assess the status of race relations in Omaha – not "fix" the problem** … The gathering of this diverse group of people to discuss the nature of race relations in Omaha, Nebraska is **a strong first step.** Many recommendations for improvement of race relations in the seven target areas have been made from the best efforts of this Commission … (p. 4—emphasis original)

The first sentence is an outright confession, confirming all that the community has been saying all along: that the subcommittee was a joke and that they were studying what had already been studied to death. By "assessing the status of race relations in Omaha," these lazy cowards relied on information and insights already studied – secondary information. If you want to know the status of race relations in Omaha, you have to interview the people who are the victims of racism, because they know where it comes from, how intense it is and what form it comes in. You don't bring together a cadre of people from the oppressor class and then claim that you want to "assess the status of race relations in Omaha." You know how those relations are because, as a racist, you enjoy the benefits and the segregation that the "status" has brought to you and your family.

Notice that the quote says that the recommendations for improvement of race relations were made "from the best efforts of this Commission." Not from concrete results; not from quantitative analysis; not from objective longitudinal assessment and comparison. No. From "the best efforts" of the Commission. So if the Commission is filled with people who are ignorant of race relations, then their "best efforts" are going to culminate in a collectively foolish conclusion. And that is exactly what happened.

After this confession, the overall weakness and inadequacy of the committee is addressed, in a backhanded way, but addressed nonetheless. Note the following "well-at-least-we-tried" foolishness:

> … Challenges that Omaha and the nation have faced concerning race relations did not happen overnight. Subsequently, the on-going recommendations and solutions will not "fix" the problem of racism – intentional or not – overnight … The Omaha Community must be constantly vigilant of inequities or opportunity, and be change-hardy and solution-driven about processes or behaviors that perpetuate those inequities … (p. 4)

These people are local and they are part of a subcommittee that is supposed to be looking into racism here in the River City. Why then, do they write begin by writing about, "challenges that Omaha and the nation have faced concerning race relations?" The answer is because they know that they failed but they want the reader to know that the entire nation has failed to deal with racism, so Omaha is not by itself. In a word, misery loves company. After indicting the entire nation in an attempt to ameliorate their own racism and segregation-oriented tendencies, the subcommittee then stoops to clichés: it didn't start overnight so it won't be fixed overnight.

These people realize that Omaha is a wealthy city and that racism played a major role in building that wealth. The master of the subcommittee, Hal Daub, knows that it is racism and his hatred of North Omaha that is going to generate Federal dollars for the city—money that he can steer away from North Omaha and use to improve his downtown skyline, build more places where white people can engage in freakishness and frolic, and use to entice more companies into the city, companies that won't hire people of color.

That is why all this subcommittee could come up with, after all those months, is sweet-sounding, liberal rhetoric like that which follows:

> What IS needed if Omaha, Nebraska is to continue to strike to be an inclusive community that values differences of all types, is for MORE people to continue to come together in a spirit of unity … (p. 4— emphasis original)

And finally, after realizing that their efforts were abysmally inadequate, they conclude, nonetheless, by trying to make themselves look like civil rights pioneers:

> The Omaha Commission on Community and Race Relations has laid the groundwork for open dialog … several of the subcommittees have decided to continue their work by sharing and partnering with

> community organizations. Let the good work begun by these dedicated
> volunteers continue. … (p. 4)

This is the product, not of white trash or some high school dropouts. This is the work of the best that Omaha's white community can produce. This is their ultimate effort. And you see what it looks like and what it entails. And as you read it, things don't get better. They get measurably worse.

The next section of this "race commission" study carries the heading, "Overview From the General Chairs." Following is that interview and my analysis of it

***   ***   ***

Racism makes you do stupid things. In order to feign a concern for race relations, Mayor Hal Daub knew that he had to pick a chairman that would make him (Daub) appear "wise." He couldn't pick a white one because that would look like paternalistic racism; he couldn't pick a black one because he (Daub) distrusts and despises African-Americans. He couldn't pick a Latino because it might make the Blacks and other racial minorities feel left out. So what do they do? Three people are picked to serve as "general chairs." The three are Eddie Staton, a system-oriented "Negro" whose words and actions prove he is beholden to the mayor; Rita Melgares, a conservative Latina lawyer; and Roy Smith, owner of a white car franchise and a very rich man. This "menagerie," then, served as the leadership for a "Commission" that was supposed to address race relations with some semblance of seriousness.

The paper is supposed to be apolitical, but what do they write in the document? Take note:

> We want to also express appreciation to Mayor Hal Daub for his
> support and vision in the creation of this commission. We hope that this
> will be the first in many efforts to publicly denounce racism and
> discrimination of all types in Omaha … (p. 5)

If he supported it, then that means he was around when they were writing it. And if the commission was the creation of Daub's vision, then that explains why it was filled with racists and incredibly unqualified people of color. It also explains why the committee's statements, like the actions of the mayor who created it, are also contradictory.

For instance, the commission writes that, "we hope that this will be the first in many efforts to publicly denounce racism and discrimination of all types in Omaha." That statement translates to mean that racism and discrimination are always going to be around, hence the need for "many efforts" in the future. This is

the kind of foolishness that exposes racists for the imbeciles that they are. This
Commission is surely no exception.

And because they know that they are visibly making themselves look like
fools, they immediately launch a reaction formation and attempt to place the blame
on those who can see through the cheap scam that they are trying to pull off. They
write that,

> … Let the critics say what they will – if they did not actively
> participate in this process they personify the adage: "If you're not part
> of the solution, you're part of the problem. …"

The only way to "actively participate" was to be "recruited" by one of the
members of the Commission. Therefore, if you weren't recruited, what they are
saying is that you are part of the problem – as if they and only they are part of the
solution. Anything created by Hal Daub is going to be racist because that is what
he is. And those Commission members know what they are doing – they just don't
give a damn. And it is this very lack of values and morals which prompts them to
attempt to transfer the blame onto others.

The whimpering idiots know their shortcoming, and that is why they cover
them up by claiming that they have just started:

> Racism in America has existed for over 300 years. While the efforts
> and recommendations of this Commission are not a quick fix, it is a
> beginning …

A beginning to do what? Moving on, they write,

> If change is to happen, it must begin at the top! We challenge all arms
> of City and County government, as well as leaders of Corporate,
> community Educational and Religious organizations to take an adamant
> moral stand of denouncing racism, bigotry and hate. We urge these
> leaders to weave a culture of understanding, respect and valuing of
> differences among people .. TODAY! (P. 5 –all emphasis original)

This suggestion about change beginning at the top is how racism is
maintained. The change has to start at the bottom, collectively amass influence and
power, and then influence those at the top with the numbers of people who want to
influence and determine new policy. Why would a racist who has things going the
way he wants – practicing racism in full view and still not have any opposition
from most whites – stop in the middle of the stream and reverse his position? It

doesn't make sense, but the suggestion once again shows how silly the people on this Commission are.

How can they "challenge" anyone in the corporate, community, educational or religious community? They are beholden to these interests! That is why the meetings were so poorly attended; that is why of the three General Chairs, only the "Negro" member came forward and tried to justify the contents of the report. This was because that "Negro" was the only one with the tombstone courage to condemn the head of the local NAACP. Had Smith done it, he would be exposed for his racism; had Melgares done it, she would have been attacked by the Latino and Black leadership. But when a "Negro" does it, the attack is legitimized by those white people who believe that he is really a leader. But the black community knows better.

With that said and done, the following section of the "study" is titled, "Recommendations of the General Chairs." The recommendations (pages 6 and 7) are shallow, generic and written as if the chairpersons were in a hurry. Following are excerpts from some of those recommendations:

> … Organizations should create a statement of personal commitment of zero tolerance for racism and discrimination and make that statement public no later than January 31, 2000 …

A statement of personal commitment? This implies that these organizations should go to each of their employees and get a statement that they will no longer hate black people. No, what we need is an "organizational" and an "institutional" commitment and, from there, an ideological and philosophical commitment that these people will no longer practice the stupid doctrine of racism. We need financial, legislative, judicial commitments – not personal ones. If a white person never says "hello" to me in life, that is fine by me. But that doesn't preclude him or her from supporting and turning their head while their institutional representatives destroy North Omaha and then lie and claim that "the negroes did it to themselves."

Furthermore, *how can a city, steeped in a history of racism and segregation, have the temerity to issue a zero tolerance edict?* That would be self-incriminating! They would have to issue a statement against all of their white leadership, from Daub, McKiel and the County Board, to all of the banking and business interests who are behind the evil that is done to North Omaha on a daily basis. They would have to expose Creighton University and how it controls the board of the Charles Drew Center and how it is gradually encroaching northward. They would have to expose the sexually perverted and racist hijinks taking place at Boys Town, the elitist racism at UNO, and the discrimination at its malls, restaurants and movie theaters.

After the preceding ridiculous recommendation, the General Chairs continued the pattern by suggesting that,

> … People of Color must be vigilant in reporting acts of discrimination
> and bigotry promptly to appropriate authorities (i.e., -- human resources
> departments, City Human Relations, Nebraska Equal Opportunity
> Commission, Urban League, NAACP, ADL , NCCJ, Chicano
> Awareness, etc.) …

This statement was put in the report to imply that people of color were not reporting incidents of racism and discrimination. This is a dupe. People of color have "reported,""blown whistles" and "exposed" so much, and have paid such a high price for doing so, most of them are just burned out. When they do report such acts, who do they go – the nitwit who now heads the Human Relations Department and claims that a "race survey" would do some good? The same Mayor who, upon learning that a Native American child had gotten shot in the back by a white clerk, basically said "if you shoplift, that's what you can expect?" A police department that is responsible for saturating North Omaha with drugs and arbitrarily arresting black males? An Equal Opportunities Commission that is, at best, a joke?

Then, when you do report these incidents what are you really doing? You are, as Malcolm X would say, "running from the wolf to the fox." The employers who own the big companies are the same ones who backed the racist Mayor we now have. The Mayor controls the Human Relations Department and all of its verdicts. How then, can black people find justice with such an existing state of affairs? Not to mention a judicial system which includes judges who draw swastikas on reports, say "fuck you" to female attorneys, and who allow even worse "pranks" to take place and say nothing.

Black people must fend for themselves and if the Report was honest, that is what it would have said.

But if the preceding suggestion showed an abysmal ignorance of what black people are up against, the following one most certainly over-estimates the moral fortitude of this community's white population when it suggests that,

> … It is the responsibility of People (sic) who are NOT of color to also
> be vigilant in taking action when they see occurrences of racism,
> whether it be confronting the perpetrator of the racist behavior or
> refusing to patronize an establishment who (sic) is guilty of such
> behavior …

Now the board is asking the racists to spot and respond to other acts of racism! If white people had the collective capacity to do this, there would be no residential segregation in Omaha; there would be no District 66, for surely their racism and the subsequent "white flight" led to the creation of far west Omaha! Those members of the Commission who allowed this report to go public did themselves a grave disservice. Not only did they expose their collective ignorance, but they also insulted the intelligence of those of us who are out here fighting racism on a daily basis. According to them, we are misguided: all we have to do is sit back and wait for white people to put an end to it themselves!

> Have the Human Relations Department; (sic) with community groups
> (i.e., Nebraska Equal Opportunity Commission, Urban League,
> NAACP, ADL, NCCJ, Chicano Awareness, etc.) create a community
> database of verifiable incident reports by December 31, 2000 …

First of all, the Human Relations Department is supposed to be already doing this. But who are these Commission members to talk of "having" the other organizations create a database of future incidents. These groups need to get on about the business of making sure that no more incidents occur! And as for those Jewish groups – the Anti-Defamation League and the National Council of Christians and Jews – they are of no use to the black community whatsoever. They sit on our boards and dominate our lives through so-called "philanthropy," but they are just as responsible for the condition of North Omaha as their gentile buddies are. To even include them in this list is a slap in the face of both the black and Latino communities.

Since Daub is behind this madness, and since the director of the Human Relations Department is his water carrier, what they are trying to do is "control" complaints of racism so that these complaints can be more easily discarded. That is why many of the recommendations have the "solutions" funneled through a department run by a woman who knows nothing about race relations and who was hand picked and appointed by the Mayor.

Still as yet they suggest that some unnamed entity,

> … Create a process where Douglas County employees can register
> discrimination complaints with City Human Relations Department by
> February 28, 2000 …

What has the Human Relations done for the black community in recent years? One of the General Chairmen is a former director and even he, as mealy-mouthed as he has been lately, knows that the work of the Department has been watered down since the times when he held the reins. The Department is intentionally being made worthless so that it can be eliminated altogether – that is why Daub appointed an incompetent to run it. Who else, but an incompetent, for example, would make the following suggestion.

> … Create a citywide public relations campaign to promote valuing of
> differences and reporting of incidents by December 31, 2000 …

Money can now be spent. But on what? A stupid public relations campaign! Daub and Paris-Anaka want that money so badly that now they're grasping at straws. A citywide public relations campaign against racism? Where are you going to put the billboards – in west Omaha? Because you're preaching to the choir if you put them in the north or southside.

The foolishness continues and concludes with perhaps the most absurd suggestion of all:

> … Have City Human Relations host awards event for groups,
> corporations and individuals who contribute to bringing the city of
> Omaha together in valuing differences by December 31, 2000. …

The key to the preceding statement is that the suggestion calls for the Human Relations Department HOSTING an awards banquet. How timely. This is one way to give the department credibility that it lacks. To give this department the power to bestow awards for people who promote racial harmony. This relieves the Department of the responsibility of having to do it! Daub would be present and would give a speech; the Omaha World Herald would be there with cameras flashing. And before you know it, you've got a press release, a campaign brochure and billboards showing how Daub "unified" the city. And every entity that gets an award would represent a real or potential vote.

Secondly, why "award" these groups? If they are so "anti-racist" or progressive, then why should they be awarded for it? This suggestion shows the true commitment of the Commission: surface level only. *Pretend* that you are not racist. *Pretend* that you will work to combat racism. *Pretend* that your Department is committed to people of color when, in reality, you're in the mayor's pocket. *Pretend* that the Report you just produced has real merit. *Pretend* that the Commission you are on is actually working. And then, when you are rewarded for your deceitful behavior, *pretend* that you deserved it.

That was a glimpse at "race and reality" in Omaha. I could have written more but the hour, as the Muslim brothers say, "has been well spent." We have to know what empowerment is in order to internalize it, teach it, and institutionalize it through approaches, paradigms and programs. A key component of empowerment, in order to ensure sustainability of what we hope to implement and inculcate, is mentoring.

Mentoring: Passing the Baton

An old saying from the black power movement days teaches, "You can't teach what you don't know, and you can't lead where you won't go." Young leaders: stick with what you know. There are too many people out there who think that just because they have expertise in one given area, that this gives them the right to rule in other areas. There are those of us who have expertise in a great many areas: but we are few and far between, and the time has come for leadership to take on a laser-focus on key and core issues. That is where youthful leadership comes in and that is why this week's tidbit deals with the importance of mentoring, and while I'm at it, I'll offer up a new definition, one that is more relevant to our future leaders and their roles in the defense and development of the community.

What is a mentor as it relates to communities like North Omaha? In the organizational development game, there is a saying: "A mentor is someone who's hindsight can become your foresight." Oh, if only North Omaha's community-based organizations could practice such an approach! The key to any good organization is continuity, and although groups continue to exist, there are glitches and stoppages in some of the business that needs to get done. This would not be the case if mentoring programs were in place.

In North Omaha, many of the organizations that at one time had value and validity no longer pass muster. And much of the reason for this has to do with the fact that when it comes to organizational leadership, those who had the reins had a difficulty letting them go. A few examples prove this to be the case.

When the Urban League passed down its torch to new leadership, there were systems in place that enabled the newcomers to enter and begin to do their own thing. There was rarely a time when there was on-going continuity: new people came in with new ideas and because the board changed so much, those incoming leaders literally had to start over again with much of what had to be done.

The smoothest transition, to date, took place between the time that George Dean left and George Dillard came in. What few people remember is that during the interim period there was a man named Tal Owens. Tal worked with Dean closely and always had his back; as a result, he learned on the job and when George decided to head off to Sacramento (he is now in Phoenix), Tal stepped in and things were smooth enough to hand over to the eventual new full-time director, George Dillard.

The local NAACP has undergone several transitions but with no mentoring program in place, it has taken a path similar to that of the League. When its most outspoken and many say best, director – Buddy Hogan – served, the NAACP was probably at its highest point. Buddy served for a long time, had media outlets on radio and a weekly column in the Omaha Star, "Buddy's Byline." He was an outgoing leader and as a result when he left, new leadership couldn't fill his shoes. Although Rev. Everett Reynolds came in and lead the organization through tough times, those who preceded him had a difficult time "handing over the reins."

Today's present leadership at both the Urban League and NAACP have their own agendas and are doing the best they can based on what they have to work with. But it would have been much easier had Thomas Warren had a program or paradigm out outline the vision of the local Urban League, and if Tommie Wilson had a guideline that would have helped her move alone lines similar to those taken by her predecessor, Dr. Reynolds.

Look at OOIC. Although it continues to survive in these most tumultuous of times, is there any doubt that its long time director of 30 years, Dr. Bernice Dodd, should have had leadership mentoring program in place? Is there any doubt that each of these organizations would benefit from an on-going "Leadership Intern" program, where young people could learn about organizational development, community leadership, grant writing and networking?

Omaha Economic Development Corporation had a long history under Al Goodwin and was highly visible. When Al decided to step down and bought in Michael Maroney, the transition was quick and smooth. Why? Because the two had worked together, knew what needed to be done, and Al stayed around as a consultant and, to this day, still knows more about OEDC than anyone. But this is what happens when information is shared and shaped by those with a similar vision and vigor.

The same thing is true of individuals. As great as Senator Ernie Chambers has always been, there was no one in place to continue on his work. Were it not for the 400-page training manual I wrote, one that documents much of what Ernie did, where would the record be that would motivate and inspire young people to earn the art and science of politics using the Chambers style? What will happen to the Omaha Star if its leadership changes? What about Cox Cable Channel 22 under the leadership of Dr. Everett Reynolds, Trip Reynolds and Everett Jr.?

We need these entities, and we know that those who come behind us will need them. Since this is the case, it is only logical to have programs in place where young people can stop re-inventing the wheel and thinking that they're coming up with new concepts when, in reality, they are only regurgitating what has already been attempted?

John Crosby once wrote that, "Successful people turn everyone who can help them into sometime mentors." In this case, those who lead organizations in areas where there are important sociopolitical concerns can do no less. This is true of organizations ranging from the Chicano Awareness Center, the Preston Love Jazz and Arts Museum and Girls, Incorporated to UNO's African American Students Organization, the Nebraska Black Sports Hall of Fame, Nuestro Mundo newspaper and the Aframerican Bookstore.

If we want continuity, then we have to be willing to pass the baton on to those who can take the organization into the next phase.

<u>Key Issues for Empowerment Network</u>

As you can see in this book, the Empowerment Network is tackling very few bread and butter issues, and when they do talk about an issue like "jobs," it is in a very sterile and generic way. For one thing this part of the network is about empowering white folks by taking over the black community following an orchestrated relocation program. That is why the segment of the network that is "for negroes only" is called the "African-American empowerment Network."

That is why this latter segment of the organization has very little credibility: its orientation and relevance seems to revolve around those who area already well off. That is why in this brief section, I hope to jump start the Network and get the organization on the road to relevance. Following are a few of the issues that they can address, tackle, spearhead and, where possible, actually *solve or resolve.*

Issue 1: insurance for the poor. As of April 28, 2005, there were 195,000 uninsured people in the State of Nebraska, representing 11.3% of the population. A whopping ten (10%) percent of the Metro Omaha population, according to the U.S. Census, is uninsured. "Most are low-wage workers, work in small businesses and either don't earn enough to afford health insurance, or can't afford it and/or aren't eligible for public assistance" (Fredericks, 2005). Those numbers have probably increased markedly.

What the Network should do is get Mutual of Omaha, Prudential and Aetna involved in addressing affordable insurance for the low-income, mainly those who live in North Omaha. One of the founders of the Network, or at least the braintrust behind its embryonic beginnings, is Dick Davis, who is the founding director of Davis Insurance Companies. Behind his leadership, positive steps could be taken to provide insurance of all types to North Omaha residents. This is something that is doable and that the Network should be spearheading.

Issue 2: Taxi accessibility and the jitney stands. This may sound trivial for those who take having an accessible auto for granted. But in a study as cited elsewhere, Omaha's black community is a place where, in 1978 it was reported that fully 45% of residents lacked automobiles (Urban League of Nebraska, 1978: 20). Six years later nothing had changed. According to an August 7, 1983 article in the Omaha World Herald documented that, "Nearly 45 percent of the households on the Near North Side have no cars. So residents walk or rely on taxis, buses or rides from neighbors and relatives to get to stores along Ames Avenue or shopping centers to the west."

There is little reason to believe that these figures have improved over the past 29 years with the economy being what it has been.

The taxicab system in Omaha has always been racist and, as such, there have always been dual systems. Back in the day black folks had access to Unity Cab Company and later came the Ritz Cab Company, the latter located at 2414 Patrick Avenue. When society was legally desegregated, this did not prevent Cab companies like Yellow Cab, Safeway Cab and Happy Cab from nonetheless refusing to take calls from black customers who resided in the "urban core." For that reason, jitneys were formed in order to meet the needs of the neglected black North Omaha consumer.

So racist is the city that even whites in decision making positions allowed the jitney stands to exist, realizing that white cab companies feared coming into the black community, especially at night. Vernacular cab" is a term used to describe a taxi system that is informal. The vernacular cab system in Omaha has been researched by my mentor, Dr. Peter T. Suzuki, a professor in the Department of Public Administration at the University of Nebraska at Omaha.

Dr. Suzuki's research is based on his participation as a patron of the jitneys. He literally went "under cover" for a period of time as a tax driver for a jitney stand (where the taxis operate from) in North Omaha. According to his findings, vernacular taxi systems typically exist in many larger cities across the United States in minority communities and have "developed out of a common history of racial prejudice and discrimination by the standard White tax cab companies" (Suzuki, 1991: 123).

The Empowerment Network could stand ready to defend the existence of the jitneys and, in fact, work on ways to empower them and expand their jitney stands. This would mean employment for residents, especially those who are chronically unemployed or retired.

Issue 3: Address transportation issues with Metro Area Transit.

In April of 1987, a group calling itself Citizens Concerned About Transportation, attended a public forum and accused the Metro Area Transit of ignoring the transportation needs of North Omaha. The forum was held by the MAT Transit Advisory Committee, which claims that it "passes along citizens' concerns to the MAT Board of Directors" (Omaha World Herald, 1987)

Another layer of bureaucracy. The so-called Transit Advisory Committee is nothing short of a buffer zone between the community and the MAT Board of directors, much like local "management companies" enable rich whites to control rental housing and never have to have any contact with their black tenants – the management company does all the collecting of rent. During that meeting Ed Neil, then a member of the Committee, claimed that the committee was "the eyes and ears of the community … as far as we are concerned, we are the same as the Mayor's Hot Line" (Omaha World Herald, 1987).

In 1997 or thereabouts, Linda Stone told me that 57% of MAT's bus services were concentrated in North Omaha.

Present at the meeting was Buddy Hogan, president of the NAACP, who reminded the Committee that public transportation is essential to a democracy and should be subsidized enough to serve all those in need.
On Monday, May 23, 2004, Channel 6 aired a segment titled, "Who's Riding the Bus?" The report was horrible. Omaha's public transportation is horribly mis-managed, and the routes are designed to pacify North Omaha, but to also lend itself to the relocation strategy that takes place. By offering transportation to urban fringe jobs, the bus service aids in the "seduction" that lends itself to leaving North Omaha and moving elsewhere, closer to one's job. Slowly but surely, the Metro Area Transit is cutting back its routes. What will befall the black community then?

From the Empowerment Network could spring another version of 1987's Citizens Concerned About Transportation. This would give the Network much needed relevance, visibility and credibility.

Issue 4: Tavern and Lounge Owners Network (TALON): We have a disproportionate number of taverns, bars and lounges in our community. Why not create an organization made up of the owners of these places of leisure and create the basis for the funding of scholarships? Not just academic scholarships, but monies to defray the cost of recreational programs for our young people, monies to send them on junkets to Kansas City, Des Moines, Chicago or St. Louis? If each owner put $25 a month into a kitty, by year's end there would be thousands of dollars that we could use for the benefit of our young people.

Issue 5: Metro Area Tourism Escort Service: I proposed this to Jay Baum, then the director of the Omaha Convention and Visitors Bureau, back in the 90s when a tourist was killed in Miami. The plan would be for Network members to simply screen and hire young black males and give them jobs as escorts for incoming tourists during the summer. With the successful construction and popularity of the Qwest Center and the rebuilding of downtown, such "guides" would be an important addition to guaranteeing the safety of the disabled, the elderly and others who are "new" to the area. This idea could create upwards of fifty part-time jobs.

These represent five more relevant ideas they the Empowerment Network has displayed in its existence. Developing the committee means more than just talking about doing it over lunch with the very people who stood by and watched that same community deteriorate over the decades. What I propose will lend credibility, accountability and relevance to an organization that, based on the word on the streets, exists only in the minds of the membership. As the Christian Bible says, "words, without works, is dead."
`

KEY: AVOID PLACATION AND PACIFICATION APPROACHES

Throughout Omaha's history there have been ongoing 'programs,' 'projects,' 'models' and 'developments' that have been accompanied by the local media praising the "new days" that were about to arrive in North Omaha. Having analyzed these programs during my writing of the history of North Omaha, it is clear that all of them had something in common: they were designed to pacify and placate, not promote; they were designed to bamboozle, not build; they were all about hoodwinking black humans, not helping the 'hood.

In this section I will deal with three such ploys (there will be references to others). These are: North Omaha Community Development, the North Omaha Rebuilding Committee, and the newest one, a part of the Empowerment Network's "strategy," North Star.

<u>North Omaha Community Development</u>

Back in 1972 there came an organization called North Omaha Community Development – there goes that word "development" again. NOCD was created from a grant that the city received to deal with "development" in the North Omaha area. And after one failure after another, ten years after being "created," NOCD was found to be, as State Senator Ernie Chambers proved, an "adjunct" to the city – a kind of outpost that did the bidding of then-mayor Mike Boyle in exchange for a building, salaries and some "assignments."? There was no intention about empowering the residents of North Omaha.

On August 28, 1981, a pledge was made to the members of the black community by then Commercial Federal Bank to loan ten million dollars in North Omaha for "development." In addition that pledge included a public relations campaign that would promote Commercial's "willingness to loan to North Omaha." None of this came about, as you can plainly see.

Ten years after being created, NOCD came under fire in a January 20, 1982 rebuttal that appeared on the opinion page of the Omaha World Herald. The text of Chambers' essay well documents the role that the city and NOCD played in bilking the government, misinforming the black community, and generally playing games with community projects such as a "black fence" that encircled the old Safeway Building. The fence was removed once Chambers pointed out how foolish and racist the move was.

Now, the essay:

In "Another Point of View" (Dec. 21) Carl Tyler, president of North Omaha Community Development (NOCD) purported to respond to my remarks about NOCD's involvement in the "fence and park hoax" at 24th and Lake. My reply to him is delayed because information I requested Dec. 22 from Omaha Housing and Community Development Director Marty Shukert reached my office Jan. 7. Summarized at the end of this article, it gives food for thought as to why NOCD often assumes the role of apologist for the city.

Mr. Tyler expressed a "wish to set the record straight" because "Senator Chambers made a number of untrue statements." Rather than lay a single untrue statement at my door, he accused The World-Herald of misrepresenting NOCD and executive director George Garnett through "misquotes," "misinterpretations" and "false illustrations."

It is puzzling why NOCD made no whisper of challenge nor sought to "set the record straight" on any of The World Herald's alleged iniquities at the time of **commission;** and when NOCD did decide to object, it was under the guise of accusing me of untrue statements!

*   *   *

The allegedly false illustration accompanied an article extolling redevelopment of 24th and Lake, and NOCD's involvement. NOCD sought no correction, though it's likely that it clipped the article.

While declaring that a park the size depicted in The World-Herald drawing would "eliminate a major (?) manufacturing plant and the jobs that go with it," Mr. Tyler did not "set the record straight" on whether the jobs held are held by community residents **nor** that Canar may soon vacate, despite the enhancement of his property with public funds. Though disclaiming involvement in a "court settlement" that allowed a new face to be erected, Mr. Tyler did not "set the record straight" with an explanation of why NOCD concealed information it possessed about the new fence, and accepted misguided media and public praise for "bringing down" the old one.

Nor was the record "set straight" by disclosing that the Garden Apartments' remodeled units have been priced out of the range of those people whose depressed economic condition provided the **qualifying basis** for the federal UDAG grant which fueled the scheme.

*   *   *

Regarding the North Freeway, Mr. Tyler did not "set the record straight" by disclosing that I provided NOCD and the public with more crucial information than any other source and forced many concessions. His suggestion that I "help plan" any project that is destructive of the black community is traitorous and irrational. I was invited "to become a part of the problem-solving process." The invitation revealed two things:

(1) Abysmal ignorance of the profound political **and** problem-solving significance of my legislative success in obtaining district election of the school board and the City Council; and,

(2) An inexplicable forgetfulness of my intervention in **their** behalf to help solve problems NOCD was having with the City Council and Gov. Thone's office (from which they had been effectively barred).

From Marty Shukert came information establishing a heavy financial tie justifying the characterization of NOCD as an **adjunct** to the city. Since 1977, the city has funneled loans and grants to NCOD totaling $2,046,936. Of that amount, $32,127 was a **grant** to rehabilitate the NOCD building owned by NOCD president Carl Tyler. Another $114,000 in grants went primarily for NOCD salaries. As a **moneyless** "co-developer" of the Garden Apartments, and a shill for Greater Omaha Corporation, NOD received a **grant** of $850,000 and a loan of $300,000 at 3 percent, and a share of the **title.**

As the **moneyless** sole developer of the Blue Lion Project at 24th and Lake, the NOCD will receive a grant of $400,000 and a **loan** of $300,000 and the **title.**

The total amount is public funds. With income derived from the projects, NOCD is empowered by the city to select which persons and projects will receive funds for 'redevelopment" purposes.

Under such a sweet relationship, it is impossible to ignore the truisms that "the hand that feeds, controls" and "the servant does not bite the hand that feeds."

Now the record has been set straight. (all emphasis original)

The editorial appeared in January of 1982, and the concept of "empowerment" seems to be more about empowering the city and its "outposts" in North Omaha than it is about empowering the residents who live in and hail from that milieu. In March, NOCD shows that its allegiance was more to "policing" North Omaha than politicking for it.

In March of 1982, seven years after the City of Omaha had begun receiving millions in CDBG monies, a 12-member committee was formed to study revitalization "and crime" in the area claiming at the time that the 24th and Lake intersection was *undergoing a facelift, including landscaping and renovation of two vacant buildings into specialty shops, entertainment facilities and office space.* Where is all this?

Later would come claims of $50 million being "earmarked" for North Omaha, various "committees" being set up and promises being made by bank after bank. These tricks and traps continue on to this very day. And the list goes on and on.

And yet the city, with the assistance of North Omaha Community Development, continued purchasing huge chunks of North Omaha – especially North 24th Street – and continued to act in ways not particularly in the best interests of the black community.

For instance, the July 15, 1982 edition of the *Omaha Star* carried an "Open Letter to the Community," written by Woodrow Benford, Sr., regarding bringing in more police to the area! Most of what Benford writes in the letter that follows is incorrect, but it becomes clear that grant monies were available to "police" the black community and North Omaha Community Development – under the guise of "Security Task Force," wanted some of the money. Following is Benford's poorly written letter:

> Dear North Omaha Resident:
> Due to certain illegal activities occurring in our community, many problems have arisen recently which affect the safety of our loved ones, and enhance the growth of criminal activities in our area, which on previous record was declining dramatically.
> The 24th and Lake Street Marketing and Security Task Force has identified a number of visible street crimes which must be curtailed to a minimum at best, so our community will not be viewed or perceived as a hot bed or crime.
> Over the years, the residents of North Omaha have consistently complained and requested a positive law enforcement policy against crimes and activities that breeds havoc on our streets and within our various neighborhoods.
> These crimes hamper the success of community development activities in the areas of housing rehabilitation and in-fill, commercial revitalization, transportation services, and industrial development. These development activities must go on in a positive manner, so that North Omaha can stabilize and begin to expand and grow towards a resourceful future. Crime has a negative impact on this process. So

please support positive law enforcement to assure community growth to prosperity.

However, street crime such as gambling, drugs, illegal solicitation and sales, traffic blocking, drinking, and disrespectful use of person and language are still very visible in our community. Illegal activities of these types deter the social and economic interaction from our youth and elderly, which demises the respect and appreciation of our living environment and cultural life style. Illegal acts project skepticism, unnecessary hardships, high insurance rates, property investment and lost revenue, disrespect of citizenship, blight and deterioration, health and safety hazards, and last, but not least, an overall bad image on our community perspective.

To minimize major crimes of burglary, larceny, assault, and murder, the visible street crime must be eliminated from the living environment. A positive police enforcement policy will be initiated this summer, which will provide for a safer and healthier environment for all to conduct their lives.

Many hours and discussions have been conducted to address the issues of crime in our area. Surveys have been low key, but positive and persistent results have generated strong desires and support for good police protection and enforcement of laws and ordinances which we all must adhere to and abide by. Positive law enforcement can be and is supported by everyone, who wish to live in a safer community.
Respectfully,
Woodrow Benford, Jr.
24th and Lake Street
Security Task Force

The "many hours and discussions that have been conducted" that Benford writes of above can better be understood if we go back four months prior to Benford's essay. Simply put: NOCD had been meeting with the police all along! Then we find a story on page 4 of the "major" newspaper's March 30, 1982 issue titled, "Group Begins Northeast Study." The key areas will be in bold-face type:

A 12-member committee, including four Omaha police officers, formed to study **revitalization and crime in northeast Omaha** will hold its first meeting at 4 p.m. today at the mayor's office.

Police Chief Robert Wadman said the committee, which also includes **eight members active in North Omaha Community Development Inc.,** will discuss ways in which

police can help in the rebuilding of deteriorated North Omaha areas.

The police committee members are Capt. John Mitchell, Sgt. James Skinner and Officers Gerald Paul and David Schlotman. **The NOCD members all serve** on that organization's business development committee.

The committee will focus on the 24th and Lake Street area – **a center of attention during the civil disturbances of the 1960s** – though its interest **will spread farther**, Wadman said.

With the aid of about **$800,000 in Community Development Block Grant money,** that intersection currently is undergoing a **facelift,** including landscaping and renovation of two vacant buildings into specialty shops, entertainment facilities and office space.

A city-funded consultant's study on the 24th and Lake area concluded that **declining population, an undesirable reputation** and a subsequent lack of interest by potential businesses were limiting development.

Wadman said **crime enforcement is a companion to revitalization**; 24th and Lake Streets has a bad reputation for crime, so people would be reluctant to locate a business there.

Wadman said statistics **may** show that the area is not the hotbed of crime most people think. He said **fear of crime may be more substantial than actual incidents of crime.**

He said the idea for the committee came from a meeting between himself, Mayor Boyle, the city's Housing and Community Development staff, Public Safety Director Joe Friend and **NOCD Executive Director George Garnett.**

Any recommendations the committee makes will be forwarded to **Wadman and Garnett**, the chief said.(all emphasis added)

Please remember that a "facelift" is only a "minor change" in something. That means that all that money -- $800,000 – is going for minor renovations. And if you look at the area now – some 19 years after the preceding claims were made – the primary people in the Blue Lion Center are the city's own Job Training program. The "landscaping" did not exist, and the addition of a few benches to sit on is nil because the police cruising 24th Street hassle anyone who sits on the benches!

The seeds had been planted.

The year 1982 came to an end with major projects underway that would do more for non-North Omahans than for the residents themselves. But the veneer was being maintained by NOCD and others. For instance, an event called "Community Development Day" was held on September 11, 1982, and took place between

Charles and Seward Streets along 24th Street. At that time NOCD was claiming to be "an umbrella organization of 14 neighborhood groups" (Omaha World Herald, 1982: 8). The activity included a parade, local politicians like Mayor Mike Boyle and City Councilman Fred Conley, and food, drill teams and booths.

Neighborhood control had begun. That number of groups under that "umbrella" have not quadrupled, but the people in charge are to be found in the City Planning Department. The construction of the Blue Lion Center would become a city-owned property and would not fulfill the claim of "revitalizing business" ("empowerment"?) in the area, or the 1982 "visions" of a consultant sent to Omaha by the Nebraska Department of Economic Development.

<u>North Omaha Rebuilding Committee</u>

What happened to this organization? What happened to another one that was named the North Omaha Development Plan? As it relates to the former, move up a year to 1994, and the coming of a group calling itself the North Omaha Rebuilding Committee. It was largely made up of individuals either directly or indirectly tied to banking interests. Just because they are African-American does not mean that they have the best interests of the community at heart, but they said they did.

Individuals who try to serve two masters oftentimes reveal their true intentions by the "code words" that they use. Such "code words" were present during an "information meeting" held on a Saturday morning, January 15, 1994, at the Omaha Opportunities Industrialization Center. The code words were, "let's forget what happened in the past." In other words, these individuals knew that lenders had discriminated, knew that lenders had redlined, knew that lenders had steered black people away from key areas, knew that lenders had engaged in blockbusting in the past. *Yet these people came to the community and expected the community to believe that these same individuals, who had profited so much for so long had, all of a sudden, decided it was time to reverse that trend and begin doing the black community some 'justice.'*

At this same meeting, called an "information seminar," the banking interests were there with their black-appointed representatives at a meeting that was "stacked" from the outset. It was stated then and reiterated in an Omaha World Herald article that First National Bank would lend $50 million in north Omaha over the next five years, and that American National Bank would "try to lend $10 million over the next five years." (Foy, 1994: 13) There's that figure of ten million dollars once again: first Commercial Federal Savings and now First National Bank. Moving on.

This meeting was dubbed by Lindsey DeBerry (leader of the so-called North Omaha Rebuilding Committee) as "the result of efforts that looked into the

Community Reinvestment Act, saw the need to rebuild relationships between banks and North Omaha." What he really means is that the banks were in violation of the Community Reinvestment Act which called for more banking involvement in lending, in the minority communities. Since these banks were in violation and needed to comply in order to meet FEDERAL requirements, they enlisted the help of two willing individuals, Lindsey DeBerry and John Orduna.

DeBerry and Orduna claimed at the time that their roles were strictly voluntary. In any case, these two individuals are being used by American National Bank to solicit loan applications from the black community, applications which will be made to appear as if American really cares about the community and is doing all that it can. But their own words put the lie to their alleged intentions. On several occasions, DeBerry made the comment that the actions by the loan program set up by American National was going to "*jumpstart North Omaha.*" He said that the proposed loan program would *"have a tremendous impact on North Omaha"* and that it would have a "trickle down" effect. He did not say where the money would "trickle down" from, but we can assume that he meant American National Bank. This is empowerment-type talk, and that was in 1994 – 18 years ago.

An *Omaha World Herald* article called, "Anchor Store Being Sought at 30th, Ames," the following excerpt, along the same lines as Fred Conley's earlier proposal, demonstrates that DeBerry is trying to walk the fence on the issue and, in reality, agrees more with me than with those who support the Renaissance 2000 project:

> "Lindsey DeBerry, who heads two north Omaha
> revitalization committees, said residents must be
> "empowered" through small- scale home- and business-loan
> programs before north Omaha can support major ventures
> such as Renaissance 2000." (Foy, 1994: 13)

There's the word, "empowered." To talk of "empowerment" on a "small-scale" is one of the biggest contradictions and, in fact, demonstrates ignorance of urban planning and community development. The only thing the small-scale can produce is a small scale production--and such productions are not the kinds of facts or foundations on which to build "empowerment"; in fact, such penny-ante, chump change approaches only foster more dependency.

NorthStar

In almost every black community there is a white organization that "hunkers down" or "posts up" in an attempt to appear to be all things to all people. These are groups that are usually steered by white-dominated boards of directors but who may (or may not) march out a few key "negroes" to make the organization appear as if it is black managed – when, in reality, it is not.

Dallas has groups like The Bridge, which serves Dallas' homeless, and there are other more token groups like Dallas Can!, PMI Career Networking Group, REACH of Dallas and Pathways to Progress. In Milwaukee, funding goes through the typical means: Boys and Girls Clubs, the YWCA and the YMCA and others who organize to dominate and direct the lives of black kids. Other token nonprofits include New Threads of Hope, My Brothers Keeper and Hope House. In Omaha, there is NorthStar, an organization that makes claims of what it is doing but in reality, it is like a quasi-mission, where white college students and adults pad their resumes by making it appear as if they are "volunteering to save the negroes." The same can be said for the "adults" who are poor with the African-American Network busy hustling. Literally.

This "empowerment network" and its subsidiaries (emphasis on "sub") is an organization that is dominated by the money of the Buffett family, Susie Buffett in particular. She already has a child care center in the black community and dominates and finances the lives of three black politicians: Chris Rodgers of the Douglas County Board, Brenda Council of the Nebraska Legislature and Ben Gray, City Councilman. All of them are beholden to Buffett and would never contradict or conflict with anything she says or does. It is white matriarchal control at its finest.

The website asks and answers the question, "What is NorthStar," and here is what is explained:

> The NorthStar Foundation originated in August 2007 to focus on the critical, unmet needs of North Omaha's young males - beginning in fourth grade - with the goal of successfully building them into healthy, educated, employed contributors to their community. Since its inception, NorthStar has examined models nationwide to clearly construct a "vision" for a truly unique, world class program and facility that will provide measureable and transformational growth for these young men. With a relentless focus on helping boys attain high school graduation and be prepared to pursue higher education or gainful employment, NorthStar seeks to change lives, one boy at a time.

The people involved in NorthStar are not educational innovators. They talk of having a unique program but they admit that they 'borrowed' from others in order to get what they currently have. Secondly, at least one of the people involved in NorthStar as a board member – Council Ben Gray – has been an abysmal failure at most education-related endeavors that he has undertaken: he didn't finish college, the African-American Achievement Team that he is the head of is a joke and has perennially failed black youth, and as an individual, he has had no impact on or made any major contributions to, the education of black males in Omaha. These are facts (I deal more with Gray and his wife, the latter who sits on the Omaha School Board, in another section of this book).

So with funding from Warren Buffet's daughter (who wants to dominate the lives of black people in Omaha through her monetary control of what little black leadership there is), NorthStar is yet another white program that uses black kids as a reason to empower white folks and further white privilege in the River City. They strike at the guts of the biggest needs of black people (those needs that generate the most grant money), and then hunker down, get a large facility, recruit minority kids, stock up on white volunteers, and then someone gets to publish an article or essay about how "wonderful" things in Omaha are.

The truth-claims continue in regard to NorthStar:

> At the heart of NorthStar are five program areas of emphasis: Academic Achievement, Athletics & Healthy Lifestyles, Adventure & Experiential Learning, Arts Immersion, and Actualization & Employment Readiness. Through participation in an exciting before and after school model that places youth in a safe, secure environment with mentors, staff and peers who share common goals, success in all five program areas is attainable. Building a team of partners and the needed infrastructure to move from concept through capital campaign to operational reality is a dynamic and exciting process. With a site secured in the heart of North Omaha and corresponding building and program needs defined, NorthStar is moving forward, quietly engaging broad community support. The NorthStar Foundation is a non-profit organization under IRS Code Section 501 (c)(3).

KEY: DEFINE DEVELOPMENT IN YOUR OWN IMAGE AND INTERESTS

Poverty pimping, as it has come to be called (at least by me), is big business in major and mid-sized cities. If you can carve out an area that is considered to be low-income, a ghetto or a barrio, then you can get the Federal money year after year without providing ANY evidence of having done anything positive for that area. Of course, if you did, your area would then become so stable that you would no longer qualify for the poverty money. So the key is, as I've written, to keep somebody poor, unemployed and living in substandard housing.

That would be YOU.

Fraser & Kick begin by stating,

> Most recently community building has been framed as anti-
> poverty work with a heavy component of civil responsibility …
> Communities and residents are viewed as ultimately
> responsible for improving their quality of life in the context of
> a market economy with increasingly limited state support for
> social welfare interventions. This contrasts markedly with
> models of benefits provision for the poor characteristic of
> earlier decades, and with models of community building that
> historically have advocated for the organized resistance of the
> urban poor against market forces and dominant political-
> economic and cultural practices that were disadvantaging
> (Fraser, & Kick, p. 24).

The concept of anti-poverty is not new, but because of some of the social changes that have been implemented since the 1960s when black people decide to light torches and threaten property in order to ratchet up any morals that the system might have, certain wording has been replaced with more palatable terms. Poverty started out meaning low income ethnic white folks (Italians, Poles, Germans, etc.), and then it began to mean "black" for a while.

But now because of the way that the economy has started to gradually slide, the concept of "anti-poverty" has come to mean just that – *anti- low income*. So now white folks are back in that group again, but the disproportionate numbers and percentages of the low-income are still African-American and Latino. Of course there are poor whites: *but they ain't poor because they're white*. Therefore the area left behind is ripe for picking, and that is what the city elites are doing: targeting these areas for "development" so that their developer friends can get paid and the structures built can add more revenue by being rented, leased out, or sold.
The key is to make all of this business appear to be moral and based on a sincere concern for the poor. But the facts are what they are.

Anti-poverty became a matter of civil responsibility because grant writers started putting together proposals for nonprofit corporations who, in turn, decided to enter the anti-poverty game, using the Community Action Agency models of the 1960s. The funding came fast and furiously as, from what I could see, any organization that wanted to "address poverty" had the right to do it – qualified or not. That included churches, community centers, and even human services agencies like the Urban League. The Federal money, during the '60s and '70s, was pouring in. Names like "Concerted Services" and "Inner City Development Corporation" began springing up. As they did so, you knew a grant of some kind was in the making. They were claiming to be community development programs but were really "economic development outposts." And only a few individuals and families were "getting developed," if you know what I mean.

That is how, gradually, what the authors wrote, came into fruition as they asserted that, "Communities and residents are viewed as ultimately responsible for improving their quality of life in the context of a market economy with increasingly limited state support for social welfare interventions."

The reason for the marked shift in models and philosophy was that government listened and heard the words "self-help." It is easier to control people if you make them think that they are taking care of their own issues and problems. This meant that the benefits being provided to the poor had to have strings attached and in fact, those strings would be "pulled" by members of their own groups. In that way, if anyone was to blame, it would be the people who were closest to those who needed the help – not the Federal bureaucracy. There can't be "organized resistance" of the people doing the oppressor look the way you do; at least, that was the way it was in the '60s and '70s. "The man" and "the system" were identified by race and class, not by what was being done to harm you.

Fraser & Kick continue kicking knowledge:

> Data from the U.S. Census Bureau (2002) show that official poverty has increased in recent years with 34.6 million people now living in poverty. Of this group, nearly 26 million reside in metropolitan neighborhoods, with the number of central city poverty tracts increasing from 2595 in 1980 to 3221 in the year 2000. Residents of urban high poverty tracts were over three times more likely than those in other city neighborhoods to receive public assistance, and one and one-half times more likely to be unemployed. Over 40% of adults in high poverty urban neighborhoods do not even hold a high school degree (Fraser & Kick, p. 25).

Of course the previously described information is more than likely even worse now with the economy being worse than it was in 2002. So there is a need for these cities to "hustle grants" to the best of their ability and in order to qualify, they have to make sure that there is a low-income area that they can "target" (even the grant applications themselves refer to these areas as "target markets").

One key to keeping the money coming in is to link education with poverty. That is why when you see negative demographics, you will also see information provided, as is the case in the preceding excerpt, that the people in the area lack high school education, lack a diploma or such and such a percentage has a GED and no college. This is only partially true because when race is interjected into the equation, the concept of education and success is markedly altered. The facts show that white high school dropouts earn more than black high school graduates, white high school graduates earn more than black college graduates, and that when it comes down to experience, white people get hired in many cases, after being trained by a black person who they are then promoted over. This is known as "corporate leapfrogging" and once again it shows how "race," not "space," is the final frontier.

Furthermore, by linking education with poverty you can make money on both ends: the area colleges can increase their enrollments and this is especially true for those proprietary schools that make promises about making students employable and work on a strictly cash economy. These schools do to prospective students what the city does to minority communities: exploit ignorance and create a façade that an education can and will automatically change your life. Rooted in this belief is the oft-held contention that jobs and a higher quality of life are what life is all about and as such, the path to these jobs and higher quality of life is via the educational route. As Giachino (2010) cogently contends,

> Education is the path to success and financial stability, but
> diploma mills have cheapened that truism, and have been
> expensive for students and taxpayers. With Black
> unemployment at 16.5 percent and continuing to creep upward,
> bulking up educational credentials seems like a good idea.
> Especially given that people with lower levels of education
> have been pounded even harder in the recession (Giachino,
> 2010).

In her seminal study, Chung (2008) investigated whether students self-select into the US for-profit colleges or whether the choice of for-profit sector is accidental or due to the reasons external to the students (geographic exposure to for-profit providers, tuition pricing, or random circumstances). She found that find that students self-select into for-profit sector and found that three groups of "significant factors" stand out: (1) choice of for-profit sector is characterized by lower parental involvement in student's schooling; (2) for-profit-bound students are more likely to display high levels of school absenteeism and to give birth as early as 10th grade; and (3) the average predicted probabilities of choosing for-profit sector increase as in-state public community college tuition rises and county-specific concentration of for-profit providers grows larger (Chung, 2008).

Everybody can make money off the poverty game. You can hunker down and start up a nonprofit to tutor at-risk kids after school even without having any credentials of your own; you can hang out a shingle and offer "affordable legal advise" to the community; you can obtain nonprofit status and then beg for clothes and food which you can then turn around and give out – but only after alerting the media and letting them know the time and place so you can stand there and show everyone how much you love the "negroes." And then, from that public relations coup, you can let the public know that "all donations are tax-deductible."

So all that benevolence that you hear about – the United Way, Catholic Charities, the Salvation Army – they don't do it for free. As nonprofits they continue to get money to hire staff, pay office expenses and also create jobs. They might do good work for the poor, but all this is being done in lieu of providing those same poor with jobs. If they did that, then there would be no need for the poverty pimps, would there?

Ask yourselves: what do we need that is developmental? We know that we need jobs, but in the way that the concept of employment is being defined, it is almost synonymous with finding a white man to adopt you. When we think of "looking for job," our view is always outside of where we live and beyond the realm of our community. How can we be organizers if we are dependent upon the source of our problems to employ us? What happens if we do get hired? How far will we be "allowed" to go? Ever wonder why your leadership is so cautious with their words when they're on television? It's because they know "the boss might we watching" and they don't want to lose their jobs.

When you define development in your own image and interests, you sit down and create a wish list. You know the community and what it needs, and you know that before all these grant programs, social service buildings and other "projects" came into our community, the community not only fared better but it looked better. We got by and the "underground economy" went a long way toward establishing security in our community. We settled our own problems and we didn't have the high rate of homicide that we do today. We can and must do better and it begins by looking internally and then building outward.

KNOW YOUR ENEMY

From time to time you'll see an ad or promo addressing, "The future leaders of tomorrow." In reality, that is redundant. But unbeknownst to the illiterates who make money pawning off such distortions as 'cutting edge appeals,' even a mistake in action can produce, somewhere along the line, something positive.

"Future leaders of tomorrow," in the context of this series places the emphasis on the term, "future leaders." What I mean is that they lead the future; they pave the way, define the social realities that, in turn, will lead to a better life for those who need help the most. This week's information deals with some leadership concepts that you will run into from time to time.

<u>Internal Opposition: Provocateurs and Race-Traitors</u>

Over the years, those of us with superior intellect have used that knowledge to create a kind of "hierarchy of consciousness." I'll take the heat although others have also done it: we have wrongly insulted Uncle Tom in our attempts to define those of us who we, as leaders, believe have "sold out" or in some other way, "betrayed" the race.

To begin with, those of you who read the Harriet Beecher Stowe's book, *Uncle Tom's Cabin* (oops! Sorry. I mean those of you who, out of fear of books, saw the movie that starred Avery Brooks). The term was coined after that to mean someone who sold black folks down the river – but why? Uncle Tom, in the end, chose death rather than snitch on the enslaved black folks that had escaped.

But the name refers to his actions: smiling for the master, scratching his head, kowtowing to curry favor, laughing when nothing was funny. This was the behavior that the other enslaved folks looked at with disdain and behavior that would later be emulated by the likes of Mantan Moreland, Stepin Fetchin and to a lesse extent, "Rochester" Anderson. But in the latter case, it was for laughs and the appeasement of Anglos.

"Tomming" was a survival tactic. But here is what no one wants to write or talk about as it relates to the education of our future leaders: I have found that there is a direct correlation between the amount tomming you have to do and the amount of ability and intelligence that you have. Put simply, if you're a moron, then you have to tom a lot in order to get in, get ahead or, as we used to say, "get over." But if you have ability, and you have some semblance of consciousness, you can put yourself in a position where you can not only survive, but also do so with some semblance of dignity while at the same time caring for your families.

Case in point: black women. Now although the term for them is "Aunt Jemima" (who never sold out anyone but was a creation of some pancake people), it is clear that over the years they have played a major role in the survival of black people. During that time they have had to endure untold horrors of working for Anglos in their homes, serving as nannies and the like. They had to smile, laugh and listen to others poke fun at sometimes even watch as Anglos harmed or killed black people. From slavery to the present, this has been the case.

Does that make them "toms"? No. But what they did was in the way of survival. What we have to look at is just how important is what we do to the end result of caring for those we care about? Young leaders have to get other people of color to ask, "is this tommin' necessary"?

Those of us who have our own businesses or intellectual ability have to worry about this less. But in my case (others can pretend they never did it) I have used that term far too often to describe black folks who were simply trying to eke out an existence. Did they betray the race? Did they humiliate black folks? No. And here's why: these kinds of folks are not the exception – they are the RULE!

That's right, I said it: black people, in general, are "toms." I used to get phone calls from people telling me that Senator Chambers was wrong for calling black people Uncle Toms. But I agree with Ernie: look at what we've produced as a race. That is how you judge a group: what do they, as a collective, produce that, in turn, can help them with their own growth and development? When you ask that question you come to a very simple answer: *nada.*

Don't get me wrong, we built this country and we've made others great. But those strong and smart enough to bake the pie should be astute enough to see that once the pie is finished, they deserve at least a slice of it! Our people have "tommed" and, at one time, it may have been a survival tactic. But today, in 21st century America we do it for one reason and one reason alone: because its comfortable and it feels good.

We have gotten away with doing nothing for so long that when somebody does something, we take offense to it. Like our former slavemasters, we look at that person with disdain-and-how-dare-you and work to isolate ourselves from him or her. You've seen it before. The same people that smile in your face and say "good job" when outsiders aren't looking are the same ones that are running back and currying favor, joining their bosses in "dealing with those militants" and those "rabble-rousers."

Tomming is not unique to us. White folks (the original toms) have it down to a science, especially in corporate America. They call it, "brown nosing." I've seen it, and it is hilarious. What is funny is that those who do it share the same fate as the blacks who do: those in power, because of the 1960s and the consciousness that we ushered into existence, know when someone is tomming! It used to fool them; now, for the most part, it no longer does.

So what's the purpose?

If we don't need it in order to survive, then why do it? Furthermore, if we do need to do it in order to survive, maybe we're in the wrong business. Maybe if you have to tom to get a good grade or a degree, or if you have to tom to keep your job or get that promotion, maybe you don't deserve any of it. Maybe all those black people laid their lives down or put those lives on the line so that future generations wouldn't HAVE to tom any more. The early toms knew how degrading the act was, but in the name of future generations, did it so that we wouldn't have to. Feel me?

Understanding now that denunciation rarely leads to definition, I share my information with young folks. Of course I still "dog" people that I think aren't doing what they should be. But just write it off as a personality quirk of mine, but a political necessity for future leaders.

One last thing: you can create more etymologically correct terms whenever and wherever you choose. Rather than using either "Uncle Tom" or "Aunt Jemima," I created the term "Gungamima." Gunga Din was a man in India who sold out his people to the British and when he died, they paid him the ultimate compliment by saying that he had, "a white heart." His betrayal led to the slaughters of tens of thousands of his people. So we take his first name ("Gunga") and add to it that ending of "Jemima," and we come up with a gender-neutral term to be used to those, male or female, who act in a way that embarrasses, humiliates or in some other way harms black folks. "Gungamima."

So remember: if you've got skills, tomming is less of a necessity. In 21st century America, we need to look inward because we have communities that dominate most cities and with numbers usually comes power. The fact that we are still lagging in the power category clearly shows that in the final analysis, tommin' don't work.

They put a "negro" who is a former police chief in charge of the Nebraska Urban League. The leadership of the local NAACP rotates regularly and none of them have developed anything even remotely resembling a 5- or 10-year plan. The Omaha Opportunities Industrialization Center died out when its long-time leader passed away and wasn't doing much even under her leadership. The black church does nothing but collect money and promote bullshit promises which is why there are 116 of them in the North Omaha area alone (there are 458 all told throughout the greater Omaha metropolitan area).

The African-American Empowerment Network is controlled by the money of a rich white woman who is the daughter of Warren Buffett. Other than that, two black nationalist leaders remain and everybody knows who they are. One is in the system serving as a productive state senator and the other one is repelling in defiance and self-determination the vile and vulgar images and assertions that are regularly imposed on North Omaha by the white majority.

And that's about it.

Leaders of the future, this is important information. Our numbers are too small to be throwing anybody away. Those that will leave will do so on their own. In the meantime, it is up to us to close ranks, educate ourselves and remember the words of George Jackson: "Every sickness ain't death, every good-bye ain't gone, and every big man ain't strong."

To be continued …

External Opposition: Read and Study the Words of Elites

The elites are the people that run Omaha; some of them are elected and others are not. The ones with the money control the ones who have political office, but the ones in political office are the ones who tend to commit their plans, views and values onto paper. And this is what you must study and read in order to have the keys to real empowerment.

As a case in point I now share with you an analysis of a a 2004 speech by former Mayor Mike Fahey. Study well and you will see how men of his ilk distort the truth, boast of what "will be," and tend to ignore issues of race and class.

In a word, for a long time, the City of Omaha has been playing cosmetic games with Federal money while the urban core suffers because of the lack of essential infrastructure repairs, jobs and job development, and relevant social services. This cannot be seen more plainly than when one reads the words of current mayor Mike Fahey, the most recent in a long line of city leaders who have ignored the infrastructure needs of Omaha while concentrating on downtown, the far west, the southwest and mid town areas of the city.

The Geo-Politics of Community Growth: Mayor Mike Fahey's January 2004, "State of the City Address"

Two things can be gleaned from Mayor Mike Fahey's "State of the City Address," delivered in January of 2004. The first thing is that like former University of Nebraska at Omaha Chancellor Del Weber, he is a "bricks and mortar" man. Weber, during his decades as the leader of the city's largest university, flopped in the area of human relations, but was able to spearhead the construction of buildings all over campus. That then, was his legacy: bricks and mortar over bodies and morality. The same can be said for Mayor Mike Fahey, as you will see in the following speech.

Secondly, as a result of the first character flaw, Fahey's own words make it clear that what is being done to other parts of the city of Omaha is not being done in the area where the most help is needed. Following are excerpts from Mayor Mike Fahey's January 5, 2004 "State of the City Address."

The Mayor begins:

> In Omaha's early days, life centered on the Missouri River.
> However, as we grew west, north and south over the years
> the river became less important. But 2003 marked a
> significant change when Omaha returned to its roots to build
> a prosperous modern future. And national media – from
> outlets like the New York Times. Washington Post, Chicago
> Tribune and Kansas City Star – are not only writing about
> Omaha's recent success, but one actually called on their
> local government leaders to look at Omaha as a model for
> downtown renewal.

Fahey begins by claiming that life began on the Missouri River, and as can be expected, links Omaha's early nexus to that which is geographic. But the fact of the matter is that is not the case. Omaha's early beginning centered on relocating American Indians following the incursions of white military officers who invaded this area and slaughtered countless tens of thousands of natives. This is how Omaha started: conceived in violence and dedicated to the proposition that all white men are created equal.

He claims that as the city grew, the river became less important. That again, is a geographic statement because the mayor, in speaking for his fellow whites, shows that the river area – which includes the black community – was neglected. His claim of "growth" to the west, north and south omits the manner in which that growth takes place. And he also forgets to mention that the "we" and the "our" is in reference to white folks. They expanded and then in the 1960s, ran from black folks, and created their own communities. You can not "forget" about the river and not also forget about the people who live nearest to it: black folks and low-income whites. If Omaha was located in the South, this area of the city that Fahey is talking about would be called "the bottoms."

One thing about these racist mayors that Omaha elects to office is that they all try to make that life is mute until they come along and take care of what should have been taken care of all along. In Fahey's case, 2003 supposedly "marks a significant change." For whom? His white business buddies and his political cronies, that's who. Fahey opened the gates for business encroachment and the continued abuse of federal block grant money, continuing the legacy and method of operation established by former Mayor Hal Daub.

Fahey talks of Omaha "returning to its roots." This is a racist statement, because Omaha's roots are the roots of people who love the water, but they don't love the people who live near it. To make such a claim makes it appear as if white folks returned to the east side. That is a lie. They come back to the area for freakishness and frolic, for leisure and drunken pleasure. Then they return to their western suburban homes. Like Fahey, these white people want nothing to do with any area of the city that is close to the black community. They will party there and socialize there, but only because they know they won't be there long. Most Omahans share the racial mentality and sophistication of whites in the Deep South during the 1920s.

Fahey's examples of success are geographic and architectural. He knows that he can boast of no level of sophistication on the part of his white cohorts, because they are the racists who maintain black subjugation. When Fahey talks about the national media and the coverage of Omaha, he has to qualify the statement with the fact that these media are looking "at Omaha as a model for downtown renewal."

First of all, that is a lie. Omaha steals its ideas from Kansas City and Denver. There is nothing unique about what is going on downtown because the people in the planning department are white boys who couldn't cut it in any other city. One of the former members didn't even have a college degree and was a manic depressive on meds making decisions that involved millions of dollars. *Omaha does its city planning based on racist whim and business objectives;* there is little concern for providing jobs and even less concern about working WITH people of color. It seems that all the city administration knows is IMPOSITION.

So he brags about downtown and its buildings because there is nothing he can say about culture or race relations because Omaha scores a big fat zero in those areas; imagine, a hick town with no gas stations downtown, no night life and whose businesses shut down at 9:00 at night!

Fahey's fabricated fantasies continue has he continues his foray into the world of "bricks and mortar:"

> Together, we cleared away an overgrown, littered riverfront and created a new and welcoming gateway to our city. Abbott Drive and 10th Street now boast new perspectives on downtown Omaha's blossoming cityscape and connect the airport to our main business district to some of our world-class attractions such as the zoo and Laurentzen (sic) Gardens. Gallup University opened our business and so did the Qwest Center Omaha, Union Pacific's new headquarters continues to take shape and joins First National Bank's tower in our skyline. While brand new, it's already hard to imagine our city without them.

Fahey has selective memory. That "overgrown, littered riverfront" was cleared away until those white people saw that other cities were making money from THEIR riverfronts. For so long, that riverfront was considered a part of the ghetto, and was used as nothing more than a dumping ground for some of Fahey's white corporate friends.

Fahey talks about the "gateway to our city." That Gateway, as he calls it, tears right through North Omaha if you head north from the airport. That Gateway, as he calls it, used black poverty-generated CDBG funds to make way for expanding Abbott Drive. That Gateway, and its Pearl of Lights cost more than this mayor has spent on sidewalks, lights or sewers in the black community, which is less than three miles away from that "gateway." What they've done is build AROUND North Omaha while all the while using the Federal funds that black poverty generated.

Fahey talks about connecting the airport to their main business district. It is not their main business district. What he means is "central business district." The main business district is no longer downtown; it is west, and well he should know.

He talks of world class attractions like the (Henry Doorly) zoo and the Lauritzen Gardens. This proves that while he is willing to spend money on those attractions that are already stable, he is intentionally abandoning the deteriorating area that is a few scant miles from his City Hall offices. If this isn't the "triage approach," then show me what is.

Like his predecessor Daub, he seems more concerned about the city's skyline than he is about the area just north of where that skyline is located. Fahey has done nothing in or for the black community, and yet this is the community that ushered him into office (he only beat Daub by 700-odd votes). And he repays us by appointing black Uncle Toms (Chris Rodgers, Reginald Young, and Gail Thompson, to name but a few) and doling out some chump-change grants for neighborhood projects.

He had the nerve to say, in regard to the National Bank Tower, the Qwest Center and the new Union Pacific Headquarters that, "while brand new, it's already hard to imagine our city without them." Buildings. Concrete. Steel beams. Glass. This is what this white man is about. He wants to leave a legacy of architecture just as Daub did. But when it comes to the concerns of the black community, he is so beholden to the business community that even if he wanted to do something, he couldn't. After all, the white business owners and their corporate counterparts are in bed with the City of Omaha, Creighton University and the University of Nebraska-Omaha in the encroachment upon North Omaha. They write grants documenting black poverty, then spend the money on their "whites-only" programs and projects. THIS then, is the Fahey legacy.

He continues with his geopolitical and architectural descriptions of is "vision:"

> Soon the Hilton Omaha will open its doors to convention goers and secure its place as our city's flagship hotel. The Missouri River Pedestrian Bridge will span the river redefining Omaha again, and will be the first pedestrian bridge in the nation to link two states. Riverfront Place will introduce Omahans to a brand new kind of urban living with high-rise condominiums and town homes with a spectacular view of downtown and the river.

The Omaha Hilton was built despite a controversy that included Council member arguing about whether or not it was the best one to choose from. But since it was built, the local media has joined in with covering up the realities of the building, including a recent news report by WOWT-Channel 6. During that report, it was announced that the Hilton had just received "a four diamond rating" and the report made it appear as if this was the top award that existed. After checking, I found out that, just like the "star' rating system, "four diamond is not top of the line – five diamond is.

So the Hilton is not a top rated hotel, but since Fahey has claimed it is the city's flagship hotel, it is clear that once again, Omaha shows that it is accustomed to glorifying its mediocrity, in much the same way that it covers up the racist employment policies of its new buildings: few blacks working at the World Herald's Freedom Center, the Qwest Center, the Union Pacific headquarters or the First National Bank Tower (except as janitors and cooks, just like it was in the 1940s).

The Missouri Valley Pedestrian Bridge was no major deal, and while wihte folks can boast that it is the only bridge in the nation to link two states, that is probably because other states are above such trivial and foolish "firsts." Perhaps other states are working to spend money on its low-income communities, and not on silly walkways to appease suburban white folks who don't live anywhere near where the bridge was built. This is the kind of crap that Fahey boasts about while covering up the long-time neglect of the state of Nebraska's largest African-American community.

Then it's back to the river again as he talks about the construction of Riverfront Place, which he claims will usher in a "new kind of urban living with high rise condos and town homes." See how these silly white men think? They don't have the size to be considered an urban city, but they want to pretend that they are. Cursed with backward thinking hicks and political hacks who gamble, take bribes and switch parties on a whim, Omaha is a joke across much of the country. Fahey, like other uninformed white folks, think that "urban" can be defined by the housing stock. He thinks that condos and town homes will give these hicks some kind of urban sophistication. But he is wrong. The racist and countrified attitude that these white folks have will forever consign them to a category of hillbillies. And all the condominiums and all the annexations in the world won't change that.

Finally, note where Fahey speaks about the "spectacular view of downtown and the river." This was what it was all about all the time. These white people, cowards who fled the area when black people started moving into the area, now want to return to the area. They want that view and they want access to the river, but more importantly than all that, they tire of the long commute from downtown (where there are supposedly 25,000 jobs) to the suburbs. These people want to return and have access to the lovely boulevards and flat land that North Omaha has more than enough of. They want proximity to the airport (although the North Freeway, which was built through the heart of the black community, was built to accommodate them so they could get from their suburban homes to Eppley Airfield). So even as they crave the "return to the riverfront" (which is, by the way, their slogan), they are also engaged in a strategy to relocate as many black people as they can to the urban fringe.

The Mayor's address continues:

> Our task now is to build upon the great momentum generated by riverfront work. Like our public private partnerships, we must refocus then drive and ambition that rebuilt the Missouri Riverfront, capture its energy and push it into our neighborhoods and smaller business districts. We're doing just that with successful neighborhood programs and focused economic development plans. Omaha's neighborhood remain a priority and great work is happening throughout the city through tour Neighborhood Grant Program, our residential street resurfacing program and the Neighborhood Parks and Libraries Renovation Plan.

More about the Riverfront – but nothing about the people who live closest to it who they have ROBBED of millions of dollars in Community Development Block Grant funds since 1975. And even before that, they abused and pocketed and benefited from urban renewal monies, Model Cities funds as well as Urban Development Action Grants, Small Neighborhood Action program grants, and today its Community Service Block Grants, Weed and Seed Funds, Project Safe Neighborhoods and other monies that do more to employ white folks than to assist the low income. The Riverfront is one more way for these people to build for the sake of fun, frolic and leisure at the expense of those holed up in the black community.

Fahey uses code words like "private partnerships," and "focused economic development" as ways to explain how these greedy white people monopolize all the money, build and demolish at a whim, are able to receive the backing of banks and other lenders without a whim, and yet, even amid all this, they still despise black people so much that once a project is built on the eastern fringe of the black community (that is where the "riverfront" is), these racists won't even hire any.

The duplicitous Fahey boasts about his Neighborhood Parks and Libraries Renovation Plan, and yet when it came to the library that serves the black community – the Charles Washington Library – there was no real "plan" on what to do with the books while the building was being remodeled. A last minute idea meant that blacks would be going to the nearby Benson Library, a library that had been modeled long ago even though it served fewer people than the Washington Library did. The black community is once again coming last for services: last to get cable TV hookups, last to get caller identification and other phone services, last to get its library repaired. Fahey didn't start this tradition; he simply perpetuated it.

From there, he stoops to outright lying. Check it out:

> We awarded 40 grants to neighborhood associations in the
> past two years. While these grants are relatively small -
> $5,000 or less – they've made a tremendous impact on our
> city's neighborhood communities. From banners to
> landscaping, from signage to safety lighting many areas of
> Omaha re visibly improved. I hope to be able to expand both
> the size and number of grants in the future.

When Fahey says that the grants are "$5,000 or less," he is being generous. In 2002, when Fahey awarded the first of the Neighborhood Improvement Grants, he only set aside $85,000 from the general fund. Of the twenty four Omaha neighborhoods that received grants in 2002, only ten of them were North of Dodge Street (the black community and its fringe). Those groups were Belvedere Point Neighborhood ($5,000), Bemis Park Neighborhood ($5,000), Benson Neighborhood ($3,505), Central Park ($1,500), Conestoga Place Homeowners ($1,500), Dundee Memorial ($2,500), Dundee Neighborhood (*$2,500), Florence Futures Neighborhood ($4,240), Gifford Park ($3,065), Miller Park-Minne Lusa ($1,800). (Omaha Star, 2002: 1).

These ten neighborhoods, either in or close to the black community, have a total of $30,550. This averages out to just over $3,000 per organization. But with the other 14 groups who were awarded sharing a combined total of just under $55,000, we can see where Fahey's interests are. Not with the poor neighborhoods with zip codes like 68111, 68110 or 68104, but on the midtown and white areas. In fact, even of those north of Dodge, perhaps the most racist of the neighborhood groups, Dundee, received two separate grants, one under "Dundee Memorial" and the other under "Dundee Neighborhood." Furthermore, Florence Futures, Bemis Park and Miller Park have some blacks, but these are mainly white focused neighborhood groups.

These facts send a direct message to black folks regarding Fahey's "vision." As he said in August of 2002, "I am proud of this program and look forward to the results" (Omaha Star, 2002: 1).

Furthermore, there was no "tremendous impact" made on any neighborhoods that are located in the black community. That chump change that was doled out came from black people's money in the first place! Fahey is afraid of change because, as most people know, he's afraid of the black community. He had no plan on what to do when he got elected. He realized that black people were the ones who put him over the top, but he had to phone up several community leaders to ask who he should appoint! That shows that when it comes to black people, this man had no vision. The fact remains simple: black people voted AGAINST former

Mayor Hal Daub, not FOR Mike Fahey! But he's shown what he thinks of black people by letting the police run rampant over the black community, by continuing to allow the abuse of CDBG funds, and by the way he's allowing Workforce Development to be watered down so that the white folks being laid off Countywide can get priority services over minority applicants and clients.

During his address, he claimed that,

> … the program has sparked ingenuity as many neighbors are now working together and building long-term plans for their neighborhoods. That's exactly what these grants were supposed to do - promote new plans, vision and growth, that is largely driven by the people who live there. I am proud I initiated this important neighborhood program and look forward to its continued success.

How can you "spark ingenuity" when ingenuity is the power of creative imagination? What is creative about what these white people are doing? In their own way, what they are doing is maintaining the segregated condition of the city. The neighborhoods that deserve the lion's share of the money – those located in the black community – are not getting any money and those that do are not getting the maximum amount. So why is Fahey lying?

The only neighborhood association that presented a real "plan" was the Triple One Neighborhood Association. This was a plan that was communitywide, would have created over 200 jobs, and would have empowered the area. Instead, he opted to provide funds for neighborhood watch groups, planting a few shrubs and other trivial activities. This is his version of "vision and growth."

Fahey has not mentioned human beings one time in his speech. Therefore the allegation about him being about "bricks and mortar" continues to hold – just as it does in the following series of statements:

> Because we blended new technology with old methods, our residential street resurfacing program continues to pave more streets than ever. This year 152 blocks were resurfaced and 35 were rebuilt in our residential areas; forth-three lane miles in our major streets program were paved. Two years ago, I crated the Neighborhood Parks and Libraries Renovation Plan to renovate 70 neighborhood parks and 5 libraries across the city that otherwise would have taken 15 to 20 years to complete.

Fahey boasts about a road resurfacing program that in reality, for the past two decades, has been nothing more than an overtime moneymaker for the lily-white Department of Public Works as well as some white sub contractors. Ask any one around Omaha: damn near every summer, during the height of tourist season, these white folks are out paving the roads. Evidently, they're not doing a very good job because the asphalt they put down and the way that they do it doesn't last very long; the following year, there they are again, blocking off key streets and paving the same streets over and over again. No one says anything to them about it, but you can hear people complaining all over the city.

So when you hear this man talk about 152 blocks being "resurfaced," he doesn't mention that most of those blocks were just "resurfaced" last year! He then begins bragging about the parks that were renovated, but doesn't mention the fact that the parks were in disrepair for almost two years while he was in office. His "better-late-that-never" approach hurt the parks in the black community the most, especially Miami Park, and smaller parks in the neighborhood. Like his predecessor, Hal Daub, he never asked the residents of the areas what they felt the parks needed the most. Daub had already ruined Miller Park because he had a chance to put a major sized swimming pool there but instead, spent hundreds of thousands on a wading pool! The point here is that this "State of the City speech" seems to be about construction, repairs and expansion – different sides of the "bricks and mortar" orientation and emphasis.

With 2004 being an election year, it would figure that a man running for Mayor would make promises about improving parks in the white part of the city and the suburbs; or, as he put it,

> This coming summer four Omaha neighborhood parks,
> including Sunnyslope, Roanoake, Fillmore and Lee Valley
> Parks, open again boasting new equipment, trails and/ or
> green spaces. Another nine will open nest fall. Planning
> meetings for another 12 parks are scheduled this year. It's
> fabulous news for families and Omaha's neighborhood and
> this work will continue on schedule.

When Fahey talks about "Omaha's families," he is not talking about the black or Latino families. He, like other whites who think that their values and views are representative of everyone (as in, "everyone loved and will Miss the late president Ronald Reagan"), is talking about what white folks white and will enjoy. His entire administration clearly showed that when it came to black folks, this man was even more naïve and non-productive than the man many consider to be Omaha's most racist mayor, Hal Daub.

All this talk about the white areas of town and what he plans to do for the physical plant and then he comes to North Omaha. And as he talks about the North and South areas of the city, he moves from tangible and productive business and development to his plans to turn the minority areas of the city into "freak show tourist areas" for white entertainment and consumption. In Fahey's words,

> Unique economic development plans for many areas of Omaha are aggressively moving forward. The North and South 24 Street Corridors are well on the way to becoming destinations. New business and social outlets will build upon each area's rich history and entice Omahans to the area with entertainment and business opportunities. These new destinations can and will join our successful Old Market as tourist and destination spots.

Black folks in Omaha just can't catch a break. Instead of applying the regular, traditional economic plans that have worked in other parts of the city, what does this white man talk about? Fahey refers to them as, "unique economic development plans" and claims that these plans are "aggressively moving forward." First of all, the very fact that anything is being done at all is what makes the plans "unique." Secondly, the economic development plans that Fahey is talking about is transforming the black community into a place where middle-class and upper class white folks can frolic and play around. The core of the area, 24th and Lake Street, is even now being turned into what Fahey calls "a cultural arts district" and once again, in Harlem Renaissance-type fashion, the black community gets art, music and dance while the white folks get money, asset accumulation and economic growth.

Even Fahey refers to them as "destination spots." Why? Because the black community is contiguous and adjacent to the Qwest Center and, as importantly, Creighton is in cahoots with the City in encroaching upon North Omaha. You can also add Boys Town and Mutual of Omaha to the mix. Blacks will slowly be concentrated further to the northwest while white folks cordon off the Riverfront with housing (and police and security forces) and gated communities. North Omaha will remain poor because that is the poverty that attracts the Federal funds needed that enables the City, in turn, to use the money making life more appealing to white people whose racism perpetuates the poverty in the first place!

One or two lines about North Omaha (the ghetto) and South Omaha (the barrio) and then its own to another part of the city, one with white businesses and corporations (Mutual of Omaha, Clarkson Hospital, huge Salvation Army corporate sites, Commercial Federal savings, three television stations (KETV-Channel 7, WOWT-Channel 6 and KPTM-Channel 42). It's called "Destination Midtown," and look how it is described:

> An unprecedented effort was launched last year to better
> define future development in Omaha's midtown. Named
> Destination Midtown, it's a team of leaders representing
> small and big business, neighborhoods, education and city
> government. The long-term goal is a complete renovation of
> the midtown area, which will dramatically improve the
> residential and business environment of an important part of
> our city. These recommendations will be presented this
> spring and I am excited to see them.

The fact that the effort aimed at midtown was "unprecedented" is yet another testimonial to the ass backwards planning of Omaha's city administration. In most cities, the central business district is the hub, and then, using a concentric type strategy (like the rings on a target), you develop outward. Were that the case in Omaha, midtown would have had second ranking right behind the downtown business district and North Omaha. But being the racists that they are, and being suburbanites themselves, the planners have avoided downtown (except for huge buildings to shape their skyline), skipped over Omaha, the near Northside and the near Southside, and shot all the way out to the western part of the city, annexing more chunks of surrounding areas to increase their population and, in doing so, stretching out limited city services. But these people are about money: the larger the population, the more money you get from the Federal government. So they go out west and add more white folks to the city's taxpayer rolls, over-extend city services to appease the newcomers, and avoid North Omaha altogether.

Fahey often talks about "leaders" and in this case, "teams of leaders." But don't be fooled; what he really means are "business leaders," which is the group he is most beholden to. When it comes to blacks however, he picks out novices and sellouts who know nothing about the black community and who, for the most part, don't live in it. He can't define leadership in any other way but in terms of business because that's all he's about: a middle-aged millionaire with no previous political credentials. And that is what he picks when it comes to these committees and "teams." What Fahey shows is the validity of the adage that, "you can't teach what you don't know, and you can't lead where you won't go."

Just as this white man can predict, anticipate, project and foresee the "goal" of "the complete renovation of the midtown area," he could have done the same thing with North Omaha, if he had the will. But remember the triage approach; write North Omaha off as dying or dead, and then use the resources for areas that area already stable. Furthermore, the more North Omaha deteriorates, the more Federal funds you can apply for and once those funds arrive, spend then every else BUT North Omaha. That ensures continual infusions of new money for the rest of the city and also ensures the gradual decline of the black community. And a financially deteriorated area of any community is an area that is easy to relocate. The "pocket of poverty" that is needed to qualify for federal funds therefore moves from one area of the ghetto to another. Re-segregation.

Fahey knows what he's doing in terms of neglecting North Omaha. His own words prove it in the following excerpt:

> Omaha has successful business districts, from Benson to Millard, Florence to Keystone and Dundee and many more. These small districts are economic engines for neighborhood communities and strengthen the fabric of the whole community. City support continues to help these communities thrive and I intend to continue my efforts to do all that is possible.

Look at the areas that Fahey rightfully notes as "successful business districts." None of them in North Omaha. In fact, when low-income housing was supposed to be placed in the Keystone area, those white folks turned out in droves to resist it and got the City Council to continually 'revise' the plan and then STILL found it unacceptable. Their visions of "hordes of Negroes" coming into their lily-white area is at the root of their resistance, but they lie and claim that it's a matter of population density. In many cases these are the same white folks that lived in communes during the 1960s and you don't get much more "dense" than that! But of course, their true concerns are racial in nature, Fahey knows it, but does nothing to address it. His laissez-faire approach aids and abets these racists in their segregationist tendencies. As he put it, "City support continues to help these communities thrive" and thrive they shall – with as few blacks involved as possible

These white mayors want to re-name the black community so as not to remind themselves of THEIR role in the historical neglect that has been a triage approach to community development. For instance, look at how Fahey describes the area:.

> The renovation of the North Downtown area is also under way., Nestled between the Missouri Riverfront, Downtown Omaha and Creighton University, the area's fantastic development potential is clear and will again be shaped with key community input. This part of North Omaha has long been neglected and now has an outstanding and exciting future.

The "North Downtown area"? What is that? Based on the way that white folks are encroaching on the area, they are talking about as far north as Cuming. This is where Creighton University establishes the northern boundary. Of course, they are encroaching into the urban core, but they do not want to consider that as a part of downtown, although the black community is contiguous to this area.

The fact is, by calling it "North downtown," Fahey is showing how racist he and his planning department really are. They want to designate that they are not going to include North Omaha as part of the plans for the future; they are not going to include North Omaha as part of the plans for development. While linking Creighton University to their plans, even the ignorant Fahey has to acknowledge that, "This part of North Omaha has long been neglected and now has an outstanding and exciting future." Why? Because the white man has decided to seize control of that future.

By undermining, under-funding, rejecting and stealing black-initiated paradigms and proposals for community development, the white man now comes in with his plans, plans that do not include the areas residents. He builds in the area, but has no blacks on the construction teams; he plans for the area but includes no blacks that live in the area or have background in urban planning; he develops in the area but only consults those blacks who have money as their primary motive, rather than the long-term well-being of the black community. And it is taking place and the black community's residents remain as poor as they were back in 1975 when the city of Omaha first received Community Development Block Grants. There is only one reason why this could be the case in the face of more than $140 million in CDBG funds received and all the promises made: *black community deterioration and residential degradation is by design.*

Lies containing the words "exciting future," "bright future," "bright horizon" and the like have been uttered before and are well documented, When it comes to the neglect and denial of North Omaha and its citizenry, the game remains the same even while the players themselves may change. In the final analysis, the overview and supervision of any project or paradigm will be linked to ways to empower and enrich white folks. As Mayor Fahey put it,

> And all these economic development plans and studies will be
> tied together in a new citywide initiative regarding the future
> development of our community called Omaha By Design.
> Another unique collaboration between our public and private
> sectors.

The key words of their silly phrase is "by design." It is "by design" that black people remain segregated. It is "by design" that black people are the most unemployed segment of the economy. It is "by design" that the black infant mortality rate is three times what it is for whites. It is "by design" that these people have stolen more than $140 million in Community Development Block

Grant money from North Omaha since 1975. And as you can see, Fahey admits it. This is the Omaha they want, the Omaha they're looking to improve, and the Omaha that in no way includes black people – other than as a class to be exploited and jailed. The proof is in the pudding.

And in this "design," where black people are so blatantly abused, the City is involved in what could be called "partners in paternalism." Included in that group are Creighton University, the University of Nebraska at Omaha, Metropolitan Community College, Mutual of Omaha, The Omaha World Herald, Union Pacific, the Douglas County Board, Shukert and Associates and a number of others. All of these rich white people make money while the area to be divided up and encroached upon – North Omaha – remains poor and too weak to do anything but wander.

If a single name is to be mentioned in a speech by a racist mayor, it will be the name of someone who is doing the system's bidding. Take note of the following passage from the Mayor's ethnocentric speech:

> Public safety offered our city some of it's highest and lowest moments. The death of Sgt. Jason Tye Pratt was Omaha's darkest day. It is the coldest reality of police work and his loss is truly beyond words. His tragic and senseless death challenges all of us to honor his life by keeping the promise he made – to work hard every day to make or city a better place to live.

In the preceding statement what you find are outright lies. And that is what these white people do; they pawn off glittering generalities as universal facts. You've heard them do it time and time again, claiming that what THEY believe is what EVERYBODY believes. In this particular case, it's Tye Pratt, the white cop that was chasing down a black suspect and then got killed as a result. And the entire city went mad! They had regular programming pre-empted on four networks, they held the funeral in a major auditorium and they marched his blonde, trophy wife out to cry out against a judicial system that put the shooter (Albert Rucker) on the streets. But they held back some information.

One thing they held back was the reason why Rucker, an habitual criminal, was out on the streets was because the Omaha Police Department was using him as a snitch. There is no telling how many black folks went to jail because of information provided by Rucker. Evidently, Rucker – as do many confidential informants – felt that he was above the law. He wasn't. Tye Pratt's fellow officer, capped Rucker and killed him.

Fahey praises this one officer and says that his death bought low moments for the entire city. Aren't blacks part of the city? All the death bought black people was more evidence of how cowardly Fahey was in confronting the issues that followed. Here, in a nutshell is what took place.

After Pratt was killed, a black minister named Bishop William Barlowe donated $100 to Pratt's two young children in the name of Rucker's children. A television show host, who is also a well-known black police officer, Tariq Al-Amin, didn't appreciate the gesture. His position was that Barlowe had no right to donate money in the name of Rucker's children, as if those children had something to do with it or as if their father was somehow in the wrong. Al-Amin, during one of his shows, held up a straight razor and said he was donating it to the Rucker children so that when they grew up, they could cut Barlowe's throat for making such a degrading donation.

Al-Amin was first, suspended for a short time and then a black police chief, Tommy Warren, was hired. Warren's first order of business? To terminate Al-Amin from the department. Al-Amin appealed and then with a wealth of community support, was able to win back his job. Fahey was nowhere to be found during this incident and had nothing to say. When asked about the controversy, Fahey said it was a matter for the City's Personnel Department. This is how "hands on" he is when it comes to dealing with racial issues – but he invokes the name of Tye Pratt so that he can curry favor with the police department.

Even his reference to "Omaha's darkest day" says a lot about Fahey. First of all, the shooting one one cop is not enough to make it the worst day for any city as large as Omaha. But secondly, if it was, why does the day have to be designated as being "dark"? Why do these white people, who lie to their children and say that racism is over, continue to use words like "dark" and "black" to describe all that is negative, hurtful, dirty or evil? It's called "meta-racism" and Kovel (1970) defines it as racism that goes beyond the every day overt acts, but indeed, people can be devoid of racial prejudice but because they acquiesce in the larger cultural order, they are unconsciously racist rather they know it or not. This is Fahey's problem: he thinks that appointing unqualified "negroes" to lead key departments is not a racist act because the participants are black. But he intentionally appoints those he knows are not qualified hoping that in doing the bidding for whites, these "negroes" will also ignore and insult the black community.

Fahey's whole approach has been one of meta-racism; the friendly smile even as he appoints a police chief who has black skin, but an apparent utter contempt for black people. Talking about neighborhood development even as he perpetuates the racist tradition against North Omaha. Claiming to want to restore unity to city hall while allowing the police department to conduct illegal DNA searches on black men in North Omaha, with vague descriptions, in the name of a search for an alleged "serial rapist." This is the test to Fahey's character. And on Triple One's report card, this mayor comes in with a "D-minus."

First, check out what he has to say about the fire chief and his appointments to the Fire Department:

> Now, new chiefs in both the Omaha Police and Fire departments have set a course that will position our public safety teams for professional community-driven leadership well into the future. Chief Robert Dahlquist and Assistant Chiefs Jim Love, Mark Rohlfing, and Jack York reflect the rich traditions that Omahans expect from leaders – including public service, leadership, education, family and a love for our city and its citizens. Not surprisingly, Chief Dahlquist comes from a family of public servants. His late father, Horton, also served as fire chief.

These white firemen are not less racist than their ancestors. Fahey, by his own admission, appoints one because of a "family tradition." But in his ignorance he cannot see that as far as black people are concerned, the hiring and appointment policies of whites all over Omaha is based on a "family tradition;" a tradition that makes it clear that there black folks need not apply. The appointment of cops also shows Fahey's meta-racism, pure and simple:

> Police Chief Thomas Warren is a native Omahan and deeply committed to public serve and community policing. Eric Buske and Don Thorson, whom I promoted to Deputy Police Chief, join him as OPD's new leadership team. To name three top managers at once was a unique opportunity, but was also an obvious choice. All three could have been police chief most anywhere in the country. It made sense to put them all in leadership positions, and I am pleased I had the opportunity to do so. Omaha will be better for their efforts.

In this case, a black man, with more than 20 years experience on the workforce, scored higher than anyone on the police tests, and was the leading finisher among the top three candidates. But Fahey and others know how fickle the white man is and they know how racist the city is. So they could not appoint a black man as police chief without also doing "something" for the two white boys would couldn't cut it. So that is what Fahey did: he promoted all three of them. This was a move that downplayed the accomplishment by the black appointee, who was to become the first black police chief in Omaha history.

Fahey needed someone to make the termination of police officer Tariq Al-Amin permanent, because if a white man did it, the act would look like an act of racism. So he selected Warren. Even though Warren had the best marks, this doesn't mean anything in Omaha, where more than a few black men violated laws of protocol to stop from being seen as "nigger lovers." Secondly, Warren was making history and Fahey would be able to tell the black community that Warren was a minority. White folks, for the most part, appreciate, but can't quite figure what an Uncle Tom is. Fahey thinks that appointing Warren is going to curry favor with black voters. But Warren's recent speech at a local library, where he all but admitted that he was in, of and for the police department, made it clear that Fahey had truly hired a "company nigger." And in doing so, Fahey has alienated himself even further from the very community that put him into office.

And yet, he describes his decisions and appointments regarding both the Fire and Police Departments thusly:

> They are all committed to the concept of community
> policing and their support will allow us to move farther and
> faster than we have in the past. The Omaha Police and Fire
> Departments are some of the finest in the nation for two
> simple reasons – they are outstanding public servants
> dedicated to our community with strong committed
> leadership.

Farther and faster toward what end? He doesn't say because he doesn't know. But the police know: they view Fahey as a milquetoast who they can run over whenever they want to, and what they want to do is put as many black youth into jail as possible; every arrest means one more black kid with a police record. Every arrest has the potential to be upgraded to a Federal charge and, as a result, to overload the prison system so that the policymakers can influence the Legislatures to allocate more money for the construction of more detention centers, jails and prisons; all in small towns, all hiring nothing but white folks, folks who are too stupid to get jobs doing anything else, so they are hired to guard, harass and oversee black people.

And more white people are needed to make Omaha the kind of city whose population means that the city will get more Federal dollars. Here are Fahey's views on mergers and taxes:

> The climate has never been so ripe for merger in Omaha,
> Nebraska. Positive merger votes by the Douglas County
> Board and the Omaha City Council permit us for the first
> time our history, to begin the work to achieve mergers and
> efficiencies in the areas that make good sense. And that's
> great news for the taxpayers of Omaha and Douglas County.
> Making government more efficient and effective, and at the
> same time less expensive, must be our goal.

This is more evidence of the triage approach, an approach that has no room for the black community. This man talks about mergers, which means and includes annexing other communities. This increase the size of the city, but it also means extending services to those areas. This is why he is going to have a difficult time making government more efficient; the more they access, the more money it will cost them both in the short- and long-term. And when it comes to merging the County and the City services, there may be some scant savings somewhere down the road, but such a merger means re-tooling, re-defining and realigning both governmental entities. It also means layoffs and terminations, which is going to cost the city in terms of paying out unemployment compensation. These people are not thinkers, but they believe that if they use enough poly-syllabic words, the low-brown citizenry will just lose interest and turn away.

In a merger situation, as you annex new villages and areas, what happens is that there will invariably be less for each area and in a triage situation, the poorest areas receive little or nothing. So what is an "efficiency" for one entity (the City of Omaha) is a "nail in the coffin" for another area (North Omaha).

Fahey's thinking is not logical; it is short-term and it is dangerous. The following passage provides examples of this myopic vision:

> It's an opportunity we have to send a strong message to the entire state. We're pursuing the areas that make the most sense. What I call the "low hanging fruit" like the personnel, parks, planning and purchasing departments. The careful and thoughtful steps taken to merge these departments will lay the foundation for larger, more complicated mergers.

The low hanging fruit approach to anything is also known as a copout. An old statement teaches us that, "all rivers and most men, are crooked, because they choose the path of least resistance." That is what Fahey is all about and you just read his own words acknowledging the fact. "DO what is most expedient, what is the easiest." Forget about helping those who need the most help; help those who are already stable and in that way you can boast about having a great track record of success. Forget about doing the right thing, do the thing that is the most expedient.

While he is talking about merging departments in an attempt to look fiscally conservative and in charge, he is also placing people in charge of departments which shows how out of touch he is. One "negro" he appointed to head the Human Relations Department cut and ran, claiming he didn't feel well physically. But he feels good enough to run his own legal practice. The replacement is a woman who is even more shallow than the first appointment and take note that both appointments are people assigned to head the Human Relations Department. This is a department that should have the LARGEST budget in City Hall because there are so many acts of discrimination taking place around the city.

But they don't, and the reason is clear: the companies, businesses and corporations who are doing the discriminating are the same ones that endorse and donate money to the political campaigns of people like Fahey! That is why he puts DUNCES in charge of the Department, people who will not do what is right, but will – as he teaches – do what is politically expedient. The same strategy was taken by his Republican predecessor Hal Daub; that is why discrimination and racist activity is on the rise. Those who practice these evils know that when it comes to City Hall, they have the "go ahead"! The last several directors – from Kellie Paris Anaka and George Davis to Reginald Young and now Gail Thompson – have no love for the black community even though all of them are black. Their collective gutlessness and perfidy clearly pave the way for calls for a Latino/a or some other person of color to seize the reigns. These four people were and are, to put it mildly, miserable failures.

Fahey's poor decision making, rooted in laissez-faire management principles, outright cowardice and, of course, token patronage, can be seen in his following statement as well. He claims that,

> Not only is it important to streamline Omaha and Douglas
> County government services thereby creating a more
> responsive government, it's critical we begin thinking about
> how to grow and market this region. From our
> neighborhood communities to our business, development
> and tourism industry, our city county and region's future
> growth, development and vitality are dependent upon
> working together. Mergers are all about working together.

As if streamlining government is going to make it more responsive (while at the same time expanding the size of the city, enlarging it and exhausting city services), Fahey's mistakes continue. He wants to promote tourism (and even has an ad on television promoting Omaha and begging for convention business), but he wants to ignore a part of the city that is an available but unavailed of source of "cultural tourism:" the black community.

These backward Omahans want to promote a city atmosphere, but they want to remain small-time and small-town when it comes to their racist values. They want to talk about urban sophistication while displaying a Snuffy Smith-like backwardness in their relations with people who are ethically, racially and ideologically different from themselves. They want to talk about tourism when, only scant years ago, they had a law on the books forbidding back-to-back black concerts at the Civic Center. SO embarrassed were they about their racist policy that they had to undo it and then issue an apology to the superstar that they offended, none other than the great king of punk funk, Rich James!

Fahey continues by claiming,

> The Greater Omaha Convention and Visitors Bureau has assigned Omahans the task of selling their city to their professional organizations – and it's working. The GOCVB has booked 114 meetings and conventions – many of those sparked by local Hometown Heroes – citizens who have promoted their city. That generates more than 56,000 in hotel room nights and an economic impact of almost $41 million for our city. In 2004, Omaha, more and more, will be the place to be for conventions.

Fahey says that the Omaha Convention and Visitors Bureau has assigned the task of selling the city to their professional organizations. In other words, passing the buck – passing onto others that which is the OCVB's job! These professional organizations may be able to convince their national chapters to sponsor conventions here, but tourism is much more than that: it is creating harmony and security so that once people HEAR about Omaha, they will want to come, no matter WHAT organization they belong to!

This go out and "convince" people to come to Omaha is an activity that might serve for the time being; but if these hillbillies want a long-term commitment, they are going to have to change their 19th century attitudes on race, on social issues, on male-female relationships and the like, and become more open-minded to what is taking place in other parts of the world! Fahey's "patchwork approach" to tourism is *one more example of his short-sightedness and his tendency toward appeasing white groups instead of attacking essential social problems.*

Omaha will not be a place people want to come to when the world finds out how this city treats its black and Latino citizens. The word went national during the Al-Amin conflict; the word got out when Daub spent four years attempting to destroy North Omaha with his repressive police policies; the nation found out when the city's major newspaper sponsored a polygraph test, using an out of town firm, to confirm a racist white mayor who was running against a black woman. The nation is aware of the rise in guns and gangs in Omaha, Nebraska and in fact, Time magazine did a front-page story on it. And more recently, blacks around the country now know about the Omaha police and the abuse of search and seizure power during a DNA sweep that violated the rights of black men all over the city.

The local media does what it can to contain the racism of this city, knowing that if they record and report it, one of the larger affiliates might pick up a story and expose Omaha for what it is. That is why these stations keep their "community focus" programs confined to the personalities of people who don't know what the issues are: re-defining a once significant program on Channel 7 (KETV) so that now it is a roundtable that includes two white conservatives and a black host who can't control his show; bringing on an ignorant farm boy as Channel 3 (KMTV) has done with Travis Justice, and allow him to spew forth his specious and spurious "opinions" on a nightly basis; airing syrupy commitments to race relations as Channel 6 (WOWT) did several years back, knowing full well that station's racism led to the loss of the best black reporters in town (Ray Metoyer, Jon McCaa, etc.); and then Channel 42 (KPTM) that lacks any black anchors, no black reporters and an obvious affinity for the grandiose and inaccurate.

This is what Fahey's "patchwork tourism" has to deal with, and it one more reason why this city will always remain the punch line of one-liners and jokes on TV situation comedies. For instance, he grasps on to simplistic symbolism and attempts to pawn it off as substance in the following assertion:

> Have you noticed the red O!'s around town? It's all part of a
> community campaign led by the Greater Omaha Chamber of
> Commerce, Greater Omaha Convention and Visitors Bureau
> and the Mayor's office to generate excitement and pride.
> This couldn't be a better time as Omaha celebrates its 150th
> Birthday this summer.

This man thinks red "O!'s" are going to make Omaha more likeable to those that the city oppresses? The people at the Convention Bureau are making tens of thousands of dollars a year, and yet THIS is the best they can come up with? Here's what Fahey should do: disband the tourism department and merge it with the public relations office downtown. He should scrap those so-called "tourist experts' because they are not doing the job. He might want to consider creating a department of "Tourism and City Planning" and break up that "old boys network" that exists in the planning department, a group of people that have systematically raped North Omaha and done nothing more than mimic and copy that which they see taking place in other parts of the country. Until Fahey makes a definitive step and totally investigates his planning department and does something about the non-creative miscreants in the tourism division, the best he will be able to come up with regarding a descriptive slogan will be, "O-no!"

Omaha's celebration of its 150th birthday was as lily white as its day to day activities. Most of the people who live here are more than willing to adapt in exchange for the low cost of living and the laid-back atmosphere. But this is only another short-term solution: Omaha's political leadership is so backward that inevitably, more and more criminal activity will be uncovered at City Hall and beyond.

Fahey, obviously blind to these facts, continues his "State of the City" address with the following cheerleader-like statement:

> Omaha is on a roll and it's up to us to define our future.
> Some may see last year's riverfront redevelopment as a
> great conclusion. I see it as a launching pad for 2004 and
> beyond.

Fahey, attempting to sound upbeat, claims that the city is on a roll, but then says "it is up to us to define our future." And yet in all his speech, he has not given one inkling, one scintilla of a piece of evidence that the "we" is anybody more than white folks. He has offered no examples of cultural relativity, nothing inclusive and nothing remotely "human" when it comes to the attitudes that keep black people trapped socially, economically and politically. He totally mis-reads his own attempts at appointing credible people and has no idea of the negative impact that his appointments have had on the way that black people perceive City Hall. With such a track record, he is in no position to claim that he is defining anything more than white supremacy. If you can see the river, you can see North Omaha; but since the river can generate money and tourism for white folks, and all North Omaha does (thanks to a racist media) is scare those same white folks, use money to defend and develop the former, while denigrating and denying the latter. This is the only kind of "launching pad" Fahey could be talking about.

He then reiterates the mistakes made earlier:

> Above all else I will continue to fight tax increases by strictly
> controlling spending as we have for the past three years in a
> historically slow economy. I will concentrate my efforts on
> merging city and county government, from promoting
> neighborhood economic development plans to ensure their
> success, on strengthening our smaller business districts, and
> revitalizing our parks and public spaces.

Not one word about black folks. Not one word about dealing with the racist nature of society. Not one reference to a so-called, no longer heard about group called the Race Commission (remember THAT farce started by former mayor Daub?). There is nothing in his own words that would make black people feel as if they are a part of the city. He avoids referring to any of the many police-community related controversies that took place on his watch. And why should he? He avoided every single one of them.

He then winds down his speech talking about something he knows little about: urban planning. As he eloquently elucidates,

> The "cookie cutter" approach to planning won't work for Omaha as each community deserves and will get individual attention. I look forward to new design standards, so that while we not only grow our city, we also enjoy the urban environment too.

He lies. Each community didn't get individual attention – unless he considers neglect a form of attention. Because under his watch, that is what North Omaha received. He was visible for some fly by night, far too short community meetings, and his flunky Chris Rodgers, made some appearances with his usual, "I don't know, I'll ask the mayor and get back with you" responses. That is what Mike Fahey has contributed to North Omaha for the past four years. Following the lead of his corporate masters and business overseers he, like they, have only USED North Omaha when it came to securing Federal dollars that were then put to use in other parts of the City. The Planning Department's so-called "master plan" confirms what is alleged herein.

More of Fahey's address:

> I look forward to continued civility within City Hall and far beyond its walls. I look forward to Omaha making a tremendous mark on the national convention scene by attracting visitors from around the country.

Continued civility? That was a stab at Daub, and one of his campaign issues; Daub had divided the city and was a tyrant at City Hall. He was – and remains – a racist and this unified North Omaha as never before. Black people, for the most part, were able to repudiate and repel almost every racist trick Daub tried to implement. He was a racist and wasn't ashamed to show he was; his big mouth got him into trouble time and time again and enabled black people to come together in rage and revolt and deal with a man who obviously had major issues in the area of race.

So the vote of 2000 was not FOR Fahey – it as AGAINST Daub. And one of the points that Fahey kept mouthing was the issue of "restoring civility to city hall." But where Fahey fell short – and still falls short – is that he hasn't restored much of anything at City Hall. His so-called "Minority appointments," with the possible exception of Cecil Hicks, were a joke and indeed, were very similar to those made by his predecessor. Fahey just appointed more of them.

Secondly, Fahey hasn't done anything to bring "civility" to the white suburbs. They remain racist and ethnocentric. They remain hostile to low income housing. They still harbor a hatred for Senator Ernie Chambers who simply tells it like it is. Fahey cannot restore something in City Hall that does not exist in the context of where the people who work at City Hall reside. For him to believe that he could and then to claim that he could, once again shows an abysmal ignorance of a man who is more concerned with bricks, cement and construction than he is with human development.

His own speech makes it clear that the preceding allegation has merit. Fahey continues by uttering,

> I look forward to new and better recreational facilities, and working closely with the Greater Omaha Chamber and our business community to develop more retail opportunities, more jobs and affordable housing. I look forward to stronger, community focused public safety teams. And more work to strengthen after school programs. All of this, of course, with one goal in mind: making Omaha an even better place to live and work.

He says nothing about location when he's making promises along social lines, does he? New and better recreational facilities where? More retail opportunities, jobs and affordable housing – in what part of the city? He wants a strong, community focused public safety team – where will that be located? He wants after school programs – which schools? He wants to make Omaha a better place to live, but for whom? And if the answer is, "for everybody," then why doesn't he get more specific about the locations of these "visions" of his, since Omaha is racially and residentially segregated?

The speech mercifully concludes with Fahey telling the city that, "It's a pleasure to serve as your mayor. The future of our city is bright and the days ahead will be wonderful. Best wishes for a happy, healthy and prosperous new year. Thanks for your time this morning.

Geo-politics, buildings, arena convention centers, concerns about the airport and Abbott Drive, annexations, merging of city and county government. All of this and not one word about black folks. The only black person mentioned is an African-American police chief who is, by the chief's own words, is concerned more about law enforcement and understands his role than he is about black people. This same chief adds that he, "really doesn't compromise on that perspective."

Mayor Mike Fahey is a benevolent racist, not the aversive, dominative racist that his predecessor was. He let major issues fly by and didn't take a position. The black community is worse off now than it was four years ago when he became mayor. Downtown, west Omaha and the riverfront might be developed, but North Omaha remains nothing more than a scapegoat for more city-sponsored "programs" and buildings that only serve to remind North Omaha of its dependency and predicament.

In April of 2004, Fahey sent out invitations requesting, "the honor of your presence as the community celebrates the legacy of Dr. Martin Luther King, Jr. with the unveiling of "Rev. Dr. Martin Luther King, Jr.; I've Been to the Mountain Top" by sculptor Littlejohn Alston." The unveiling took place on April 24, 2004 at the Omaha/Douglas Civic Center (City Hall) and there was music and festivities. King's sellout son, Martin Luther King Jr. III was present at the time, and he gave a speech that was generic and boring, which of course, is what the white "doctor" ordered.

The statue was a joke. A local minister, Thomas Smith, was used as a model. The statue shows King running (from something) with a Bible in his hand. To add this insult to already obvious injury, on the invitations was a quote from Fahey:

> "Dr. Martin Luther King, Jr.'s life was about fighting for
> what this country was founded upon – fairness and equality
> for all. This statue will serve as a tribute to his work and a
> daily reminder for all of us to continue to fight for what is
> right."

Less than three months later, Fahey would be allowing Omaha police to stop and randomly administer DNA tests on any and all black men because of reports that a serial rapist had been victimizing women over the past several years. Fahey stepped in and did nothing while the cops, led by an Uncle Tom captain named Tommy Warren, denied black men of their rights until State Senator Ernie Chamber stepped in and rallied the community behind his efforts to call such unconstitutional police actions to a halt. Fahey's inaction was approval, a direct contradiction to the claims he made during the King unveiling.

These allegations, as can be seen, are based on Fahey's own words. They are the words of yet one more Mayor who made promises that he had no intention of keeping. ***And as a result, North Omaha has suffered for it.***

Know your opposition, and remember their words because they can come back to haunt you. But they can also be used against your opposition and that is what we are dealing with: oppositional relationships between the neighborhood and the city. It is a relationship that was created and has since been perpetuated by the city, the county and the state powers that be. They sat by idly and passed laws that maintained racial segregation for decades. Then, once we took the bull by the horns and turned that state of affairs around, they went to more subtle forms of showing how they hated black people: redlining, steering, housing discrimination, employment discrimination, financially opposing desegregation orders and so on.

Study the opposition and learn. Only then can you be successful and in doing so, create a context for "empowerment."

THREE APPROACHES TO NEIGHBORHOOD DEVELOPMENT

I have always informally credited black people with being the originators of the neighborhood movement. I say this because no matter what major city I visit or live in, there are neighborhood associations in black communities, some active and some not. But the key is that these are neighborhoods that were not always black; when our people entered, white folks left ("White flight") and this gave birth to the black ethnic enclaves that you see today.

It is my belief that the formalization of the neighborhood movement came about when outsiders saw the pride that we took in our homes and that indeed, certain sections of the black community were named and referred to by area, usually the street name or the name of some monument or building. Since we were compartmentalized anyway, those in power perhaps got the idea to start a movement (in much the same way they take the credit for inventing rock n' roll and jazz) that would create neighborhoods, with names. The final word is that in doing so, the area would be much easier to define and ultimately, control.

In this section there are three approaches being defined: the social work approach, the neighborhood maintenance approach, and the political activist approach. We will begin with the neighborhood maintenance approach because long before there were these "gated communities" and "neighborhood watch" programs, black people were watching out for each other, having events and cleaning up the neighborhood.

The Neighborhood Maintenance Approach

The early editions of the *Omaha Star* newspaper carried a recurring college on the editorial page called "The Roving Reporter." This was no fluff piece; the questions that were asked were hard core questions and are surely even need of answering even today, more than 70 years later.

In the August 20, 1938 issue, the question posed was, "Do you think North Twenty-fourth street is properly lighted as compared to other neighborhood business sections of the city? To this day, no newspaper poses questions to its readership because, for the most part, they don't care what their readers think – or want. At that time (unlike now) those in charge of the Omaha Star were engaged in community involvement and as a result, they were – in the tradition of the black press – advocates and defenders of black people.

This question posed goes directly to the issue of "place framing," which is what Deborah Martin (2003) outlines in an article titled, "Place-Making: Constituting a Neighborhood for Organizing and Activism." A point where I agree with Martin is where she outlines how space – that is, the setting, geographic location, and socio-spatial context of a neighborhood – influences the formation of collective identities and activist agendas (p. 731). And that is what North Omaha has done for the past decade: provided a "culture" for black people to insulate themselves from the racism that permeates the rest of Omaha. No matter how well off you are of who you think you are – or who you marry – if you're black, you'll come back to North Omaha because, thanks to racial and residential segregation, that is where the "flavor" and the "soul" are at.

This is how the North Omaha community – the ghetto – gave form and function to a number of organizations and efforts that met the needs of the people of various time periods. In this case, the answers to the questions posed by the "Roving Reporter" provide an idea as to what was going on in the minds of ghetto residents and shows that we did not childishly sit around waiting for the white man to come around and give us ideas.

For instance James "Jimmy" Jewell, then the owner of Tuxedo Billiard Parlor, answered, "I think we are slighted as far as lighting facilities are concerned, North 24th Street from Cuming to Lake is not only poorly lighted (sic), but is the last area to be lighted (sic) and the first to have the lights turned off."

Now why would this be the case? Because when services are deteriorating, black people find out first because they deteriorate in our area first. When services are lacking, they begin lacking first in the black community. When Cox Cable came to town, the last area (hub) to get the optimum channels was North Omaha. When Northwestern Bell came, it was North Omaha that was last to get call waiting, call forwarding and the other amenities that those living out west got from the get-go.

Mr. R. Taylor of the Lux Barber Shop said, "I feel we need quite a bit of improvement. It would add a great deal to our business as well as to the appearance of North Twenty-Fourth Street." Mr. J.H. Anderson of Climax Cleaners replied, "That is the first thing I noticed when I came to Omaha – the poor lighting system on North Twenty-fourth street, and I think something ought to be done to improve this condition." Those from outside of Omaha can get a quick understanding of the disdain that the rest of the city has for the part of the area where black people live. It becomes clear right away. But white people don't see it because, in their view, black people get what they deserve. The problem with that statement is that far too many white people in Omaha – perhaps the majority – get far more than they deserve.

People don't have to be literate or eloquent to be able to describe their surroundings and the feelings or "vibes" that they get from those surroundings.

Today, as white folks in neighborhood associations apply for and receive grant money for neighborhood watches, garbage cleanup and other minor details, inner city neighborhood groups like the Ideal Improvement Club in the 1920s and today's own Highlander, Wirt-Binney-Spencer, and Triple One neighborhood groups deal with inner city issues, which include violence and crime. And again, our ideas as far back as 1928 generated questions and answers that are now being put into effect by those who live OUTSIDE of the area.

Want proof? The August 27, 1928 edition of the *Omaha Star's* "Roving Reporter" question was, "What is the best means of eliminating the congregation of boys around our business establishments?" Here are some of the answers.

Mr. A.B. Wright of 2872 Maple said, "What we need to eliminate this congregating is adequate amusements for our young people, like the whites – in the form of swimming pools, playgrounds, tennis courts, and a first class YMCA and YWCA. We are taxed the same sin most instances more than the white people and should have the same consideration for our young people in return for our taxes." Miss Annie Franklin of 3026 "R" Street said, "In order to keep the boys from hanging around business establishments I would suggest more activities at the Recreational centers and nearby parks should be erected."
Mr. C.B. Mayo of 2422 Lake Street replied, "I don't think resorting to law enforcement would e right, because these boys have to have some place to meet, but there should be some adequate form of clean amusements, like playgrounds, and a YMCA to occupy their time."

These ideas are the seeds of what you see today. While neglected by white planners, black people knew had to be done, knew what their rights were and knew that "an idle mind is the devil's workshop." And at least one respondent knew the importance of listening to the young people: "The best way is to have a large social to get them together and reason with them. Let them express their opinion and offer suggestions to find some other means of amusements. And if that would to help, then we should resort to the force of the law." Mr. Charles Walls, a butcher, said, "First you should explain to the boys what harm they are doing to the business by hanging around; and if they fail to heed to your advice, use other devices."

Take notice that the tendency is to look inward first, then rely on outside forces if need be – it appears to be the other way around here in the 21st Century, where black people appear all too eager to bring in racist cops to deal with nuisance issues.

What was just described was the grass roots version of the "neighborhood maintenance approach." Neighborhood specialists Fraser & Kick (2005) define it somewhat differently:

> **The neighborhood maintenance approach** has focused on protecting neighborhoods from perceived and actual threats … Some strategies community groups have employed include peer pressure, political lobbying and legal-juridicial (sic) action. The organizing of community for neighborhood-level improvement and maintenance has been a strategy to assist middle and upper classes as well as in lower-income areas (emphasis original)

When it comes to the low-income neighborhood associations, much of what is described above does not really apply. The "perceived threats" are real when it comes to black people: we don't hallucinate nor are we paranoid schizophrenics. We have endured over 350 years of white abuse, much of it taking place in segregated and/or separated racial enclaves similar to those now being euphemistically described as "neighborhoods." We don't cry "wolf" because, in most cases, the person answering the call – a cop, for instance – is also a part of the reason we are shouting for help in the first place.

Secondly, the idea of "political lobbying" is not an approach that we use in the formal sense of the term. Our version of lobbying, which has bought great success in terms of accomplishing our goals, I might say, revolves around "boycotts," "pickets," "protests" and the like. This is the ultimate lobbying that goes beyond the backroom deals that white suburbanites, because of their contacts and because politicos tend to live in those kinds of communities, practice and promote.

Also in regard to neighborhood maintenance, the authors opine,

> Regardless of the type of neighborhood, organizing community toward enhancing, maintaining and protecting neighborhood space has been tied closely to land-use decision making and enforcement … An estimated one-third of new housing units built in the U.S. since 1970 have included some form of privatized community association. In lower income neighborhoods community based organizations have organized against unwanted land use as well (Fraser & Kick, p. 26)

I'm not sure if the preceding statement is quite accurate. The authors claim that, "Regardless of the type of neighborhood, organizing community toward enhancing, maintaining and protecting neighborhood space has been tied closely to land-use decision making and enforcement." The type of neighborhood determines how much attention it will get from the city. That, in turn, is based on how much priority the city attributes to that neighborhood. Need may not have anything to do with it: most black communities are in need, but they get ignored anyway as outside developers buy up land and then sit on it. And, of course, cities ignore certain areas so that they will remain unkempt, undesirable and crime-ridden, which, in turn, generates even more Community Development Block Grants and Community Service Block Grants.

Moreover, the previous statements says that organizing community toward enhancing, maintaining and protecting neighborhood space has been "tied closely" to land-use decision making and enforcement. Again, I beg to differ. What these scholars want us to believe is that what they write are uniform facts and are therefore universally applicable; such is not the case. Those communities with wherewithal and a chance for immediate growth receive the most attention. This is called "the triage approach," akin to a triage unit in the military that helps those patients that have the best chance of surviving. The rest are placed on the back burner, that is, if they are ever helped at all.

Taking over the neighborhood movement is where the real funding is going. One way is by "consolidating" them all, or, as the previous excerpt bore out, simply creating "some form of privatized community association." This is an overseer that will dictate what you can and cannot do to your property and so on. This is not the type of "neighborhood maintenance" program that black people need. This is more of a "fortress" type situation, managed communities high on security and usually gated. One article I read long ago referred to them as "community of interest," where people of similar demographics (elderly, women, single parents, etc.) live in a secured and enclosed area where supermarkets, movie theatres and schools are all provided.

That is what "neighborhood maintenance" has come to: low on the "neighborhood" concept (after all, segregation is segregation) and high on the "maintenance," which means control, surveillance and monitoring. Big Brother has arrived.

The Social Work Approach

In the field of social work there is an approach known as the "strengths/empowerment approach. I would like to briefly share this because it appears to be more in line with what the black community should do and has the potential to do than these "wait for us to build another park" approach that is now being employed in and around North Omaha.

> At the heart of the strengths perspective is a belief in the basic goodness of humankind, a faith that individuals, however downtrodden or debilitated, can discover strengths in themselves that they never knew existed … No matter how little or how much may be expressed at one time … people often have a potential that is not commonly realized. A belief in human potential is tied to the notion that people have untapped, undetermined reservoirs of mental, physical, emotional, social and spiritual abilities which can be mobilized in times of need .. tapping into not what _is_ but what _can be._ (Van Wormer & Boes, 1998—emphasis original).

This is what I was talking about when I held three "self-empowerment" conferences at the turn of the century. I believe that black people are the strongest people on this earth, and I believe that of that group, African-Americans are even stronger because of that 400 year slavery episode. We may have survived it physically, but we remain scarred because we were never "de-briefed" afterwards. That is a story for another time.

At this juncture we continue to doubt our own power where it matters most. Far too many of us continue to believe that, "The white man's ice is colder than our ice." As the excerpt states, "people often have a potential that is not commonly realized." In our case, that potential has been suppressed by a society that only wants to funnel and focus our powers on bullshit activity: sports, singing, dancing and other forms of entertainment. I believe that we have latent and untapped talent that can enable us to re-create North Omaha in our own image and interests. If others want to help with technical assistance, financing and perhaps some consultation, that is fine: but they have to also be willing to practice non-intervention and watch while we solve our own problems.

To date, they have not been willing to do so. Instead, we are force-fed "hope" and "wishes" and "prayers:"

> Every community, every narrative needs a note of hope. In our own fields and our own ways, we must convey hope … Believing that it can be done, that we can move forward, that people will care, and that we will turn things around is contagious. (Hardcastle, et. al., 2004: p. 217).

There is a time and a place for prayer, hope and wishing. When that time is ill-conceived, and when we opt to engage in these actions instead of watching our backs while other people talk about "empowering" us, we are making a grave mistake, one that we have, unfortunately, made for hundreds of years when it comes to Caucasian people. We trust them and they know that; and that is why the social work approach works so well on us: they have a god complex and a missionary syndrome; to many of us suffer from what psychologist Roderick W. Pugh called, "The-we-ain't-ready-syndrome," along with low self-esteem and serious cases of learned helplessness. Combine these two different areas of thought from these two different groups and what do you have? Slavery, 2012. How then, can we believe that these "empowerment movements" are for our (black) benefit?

We are treated like children who need to be helped, like problems that have yet to be solved. As Gary and Littlefield posit,

> Although Billingsley (1968, 1988) and Hill (172) have documented the strengths of African-American families, the prevailing paradigm for assessment and intervention with *this group is problem focused and deficit oriented. African-American families are generally treated as flawed and dysfunctional units;* little regard is paid to their strengths. Moreover, traditional treatment models are limited in that intervention is *problem specific* (Gary & Littlefield, 1998: 81- emphasis added).

The same applies in the areas of neighborhood development. We are viewed as people to be "taught," "helped," "shown the way." Even the token developers that the city fronts money to and uses to make it appear as if they know what they're doing get no real respect: jive-time, small-time, color-filled projects that are usually nothing more than fodder for the white man's barroom jokes and after-dinner meetings with his cronies.

The social work approach has its positives, but not when the race relations of the players are so skewed and one-sided. Here is how the social work approach is defined by Fraser & Kick:

> The social work approach has focused on service delivery through neighborhood-based organizations ... Significant resources were provide to low-income families, including day-to-day maintenance services, human capital development opportunities (e.g., education) and opportunities for activity in political and intellectual movements centered on issues of race, class and gender ... Led by the Progressives such as Robert Wood and Jane Addams, the social work approach identified

> the neighborhood as an appropriate level at which to organize
> and test social reforms, but in many ways it left the politics of
> reconciliation between labor and capital to others (Fraser &
> Kick, pp. 25-26)

Again, their overview is not totally accurate or attributable to the neighborhood context when the variable of "race" is added.

From the top down, those doing the "servicing" and the "delivering" are not African-Americans. They may be ordering around a few people who are black – the way the Nebraska Department of Social Services did when it was closing down black day care centers a few years back – but other than that, the key is to associate all that is about "social" and "welfare" with that which is white. In that way, black youth can grow up seeing white people, not their parents, as their guardians and saviors. Again, Caucasians think in long-range terms (e.g., marathons); black folks, because of our precarious position and condition, have to be concerned about the short-term (sprints) and as such, continue to be open for tricks and scams perpetrated by "service deliverers."

The social work approach is paternalistic and insultingly dominating. Things may have calmed down in the last few years, but ask the sisters who were on welfare what those white social workers put them through. The system itself is rife with rules that are nearly impossible to follow, and even now, with public housing, there is "zero tolerance." What happens when those individuals, like most human beings, make a simple mistake? They're out on the street, that's what.

The social work approach appears to be the approach being used by Nebraska's economic developers in general and the city of Omaha's planning department, in particular – especially as it relates to community and neighborhood development planning. And here's the part where a lack of cultural competency is most clear on the part of the writers. They claim that, *the social work approach identified the neighborhood as an appropriate level at which to organize and test social reforms, but in many ways it left the politics of reconciliation between labor and capital to others.*

What was the process used by social workers to "identify" the neighborhood as the "test entity"? What logic would that make, since the neighborhood is a microcosm of the immediate community in which it is located? For instance, one might take the Triple One neighborhood and work within its boundaries, but there is still an entire North Omaha community that suffers just as much as those in the "68111" zip code! What about 68110? What about 68104 and 68131?

The neighborhood was nothing more than an easy to control area that could be used as a "laboratory" for social workers and their minions to conduct various "social experiments" on what far too many people in the social science field believe to be nothing more than "human black lab rats." This nation's history provides ample evidence that such a perception has always existed and in the scientific community persists to this day.

And where are these "politics of reconciliation"? Are we to believe that because two groups "collaborate" that there has been some type of reconciliation between the two. Maybe the black side of the equation, in Omaha, has led the whites with the power (on the other side) to believe as much. But the fact is, reconciliation is defined as, "restoring of harmony, adjustment of differences." In Omaha, you cannot restore that which never existed in the first place. The history of whites and blacks, North Omahans and the rest of the city, has been, at best, antagonistic. As for an "adjustment of differences," why would whites with power decide to "change" when their attitudes and actions toward black people, including segregation, discrimination and racist application of the law, have generated billions of dollars and one of the highest standards of living in the United States?

So there is no reconciliation between labor and capital when it comes to "others." The "others" – the ones who remain under-capitalized and unemployed – are fodder on which labor and capital feed!

What is more accurate, in my view, is the social work paradigm that continues to view the black community, black families, black men, women and children, as some type of "problem." They have coined such terms as "tangle of pathology," and "culture of poverty." Put another way,

> Deficit, disease, and dysfunction metaphors permeate treatment at every stage of the process, from intake to termination (Cowger, 1994). In the criminal justice system, clients often find their very selfhood defined by their crimes. For such persons, whose views of therapy and of all authority figures are apt to be decidedly negative, a positive approach is essential to establish the one crucial ingredient of effective treatment -- trust. Sometimes one encounter or one supportive relationship -- whether with a teacher, social worker, or priest -- can offer a turning point in a life of crime (Van Wormer & Boes, 1998).

For over a century, with the on-going racist laser-focus of the major newspaper, Omaha's black community has been stigmatized as a crime-ridden war zone with no prospects. The city administration has only acted with sincere benevolence when there was a riot or a threat of one. To this day, it is clear that North Omaha remains stigmatized, which is why these people who are accepting "collaborative efforts" from so-called black leaders do so only when they can pick and choose the "negroes' they want to have interactions with. In Omaha, most white people fear North Omaha, and that is why the deficit model described above in regard to criminals and inmates, can be applied to all of North Omaha because, in the views of the majority population, that's what we are.

This view of North Omaha as a crime zone and blacks as criminals aids and abets in the "angelic" and "missionary" vision of the social worker and the social work approach. These are people who believe that blacks have to be "saved" and "salvaged."

The social work approach is one that is more about paternalism and control than it is about helping the neighborhoods and communities that need help the most.

The Political Activist Approach

I consider myself an activist but I wouldn't use it as a descriptor because, like words like "militant" and "nationalist," you do more to scare your own people than you do white folks. Black people, so brainwashed for so long, have equated having a black viewpoint with being anti-white. Why, I ask, must whites always be a part of your intellectual or perceptual equation? Can't you just love your own people so much that you just don't have time or room for them? That is the kind of "politics" that I'm talking about: helping those that need help the most and, as you know, that means us.

According to the definition by Fraser & Kick, however, the political activist approach,

> … has focused on changing the institutional structures that are viewed as causing poverty and the declining conditions of neighborhoods … Not infrequently they have challenged the existing power structure by developing a community based upon socioeconomic "class consciousness" or based on other identities that have not been expressed spatially in terms of a geographical neighborhood (Fraser & Kick, pp. 26-27).

As usual, these men avoid the issues of race. You cannot talk about "class" without talking about race in America. Many of the poor are black and most of the black are poor – it doesn't get any simpler than that. Furthermore, and as I've always said and believed, there are poor white people – but they ain't poor because they're white!

Changing the institutional structures has not been a priority for several reasons. For one, institutions are designed to perpetuate, not condemn, themselves. So if you want to change an institutional arrangement, the best thing to do is to create what I call "counter-institutions" and deal from a position of power. Individuals, no matter how strong, cannot overcome institutions. You can cite the case of the civil rights movement, but that movement did not change institutions: it simply said, "scoot over – I want to share it with you." That is not even close to the revolutionary bent of groups like the Revolutionary Action Movement, the Weathermen, the Brown Beret or, to a lesser extent, the grandiose Black Panther Party for Self-Defense.

I also differ when they write that political activists have challenged the existing power structure "by developing a community based upon socioeconomic "class consciousness" or based on other identities that have not been expressed spatially in terms of a geographical neighborhood." These identities have been expressed spatially and for that matter, temporally (based on time) as well. Race and class are definers and have an impact on the geographic area. That is what segregation is all about: those in power take race and class and use it to determine what geographic area you are going to occupy: near the bottoms (where the floods take place), close to railroad tracks and noise, near toxic waste dumps and so on. These are but a few examples of "identities that are expressed spatially even though the defining of that space is in the hands of the powers that be (e.g., planners, developers, real estate experts, etc.)

Deborah Martin (2003) outlined a concept called "place-framing." She believes that the neighborhood functions as a site of political activism and further that, "Neighborhood-level activism in the U.S. urban areas increasingly operates in a political context dominated by an elite agenda of urban growth through civic boosterism and redevelopment projects (p. 731).

This is one way to put it; a more accurate way would to say that neighborhood-level activist in the United States inner cities (black and Latino communities) increasingly operates in a political context *dominated by neglect by the elite decision makers whose agenda it is to keep the areas poor* until such time as they can attract enough poverty grant money to relocate those populations and prepare those neighborhoods for the return of their elite counterparts (e.g., white folks).

That "civil boosterism" and those "redevelopment projects" that were referred to are just part of the smokescreen that those in power use to rationalize their incursions into low-income areas. That "boosterism" is nothing but a public relations campaign by the local media to provide support for the "new programs that are on the way," and the "redevelopment projects" are just that: projects aimed at "developing all over again," meaning a re-definition of the area in the image and interests of those who are in power. The indigenous populations, by way of other prongs of the "redevelopment plan," are therefore relocated to other parts of the city through eminent domain, scattered-site housing, apartments that offer affordable housing and other "redevelopment plans" aimed at inducing the poor to move to places that are more "in line with their incomes" and therefore leave the central city to those who want to develop it because of access to a riverfront, a lakefront, downtown jobs, downtown night leisure and other reasons.

A book titled, **Asset Building and Community Development** offers us an explanation as to why people get involved in neighborhood groups:

> Research shows that length of residence and interests in protecting the value of the home are strong predictors of membership in neighborhood associations. Having children younger than age 5 also strongly affects membership in these organizations; presumably, interests in safety and education are the motivating factors in this case (Green & Haines, 2002: 72).

The preceding definition falls short. While having children who are young and concerns about the community are important, what about the political issues? *People who join neighborhood associations are people who want to get involved in addressing problems – and prospects – taking place in the community.* Those problems are, at their foundation, usually political in nature.

Then there is the statement by Martin that "place informs social action." While I agree that this might be the case in most instances, it is social action of some kinds that define place. For instance, there would be no "black community" in Omaha were it not for white flight. Therefore the actions of those who wanted to leave the area gave birth to a community that is now known across the state as the "near Northside" of Omaha. So action precedes place, and once place is established, more action is needed and used to either maintain a place or relocate it.

This is where political activism begins and ends: addressing the time, place and circumstance under which behaviors take place, behaviors that may shape policies and laws that are imposed on neighborhoods. Any political activist has the right to analyze, then address, what those policies and laws are.

Finally, in regard to the political activist approach, Fraser & Kick opine,

> The political activist approach to organizing neighborhood community has arguable declined in prevalence since the 1970s, as global recession motivated U.S. corporations to move offshore, and the state began to dismantle social welfare programs (i.e., emergent neoliberalism). In accord with the neo-liberalist response to urban problems in the late 1970s and 1980s, the state has significantly decreases funding for programmatic efforts aimed at inner city neighborhoods specifically, and urban areas more generally … Together, these

factors have shaped current configurations of neighborhood-
based organizing, spurring community building as the dominant
strand of supported neighborhood organizing (pp. 28-29)

The political activist approach to organizing neighborhood and community has not declined or increased except in response to the conditions of that particular neighborhood or community.

For instance, in the previous excerpt, the author claims that political activism has declined. What is this premise based on? Did they conduct a survey or study? Who did these men talk to? If they are so certain, then why would they then add the qualifier, "arguably" in regard to the alleged decline? And why would political activism decline since the 1970s when, since that time, conditions that negatively impact upon neighborhoods and communities have grown worse, especially since the two terms of Ronald Reagan, the two terms of George Bush, and two terms of George W. Bush? Even under Clinton, political activism, especially as it had to relate to the police and to Clinton's personal issues, was flourishing.

What reasons do Fraser and Kick give for this alleged decline in political activism? Their reasoning is based on their claims that it was because of a global recession, dismantling of welfare and corporations moving offshore. Don't they know that "all politics is local"? Don't they know that the issues they've raised are moot when it comes to the low income because, for the most part, low-income minorities are always living in a "depression" or a "recession." The end to welfare did not hurt, because the money is still coming (if you can find a job), and so is the Section 8 housing subsidy and the food stamps. Poor people are not panicking because they've always been poor; political activism is not waning because the people they advocate for, those same low-income people, remain poor and in need of a voice!

Community-building, as they call it, is a term that places the macro- above the individual needs of residents. How can you build a community without first of all focusing on the individuals, families and neighborhoods that make up that community? Community-building sounds good, but it exists only on the aerial maps and drafting tables of urban planners. They can talk about it in such generic terms because the impact of what is taking place in those neighborhoods and communities *does not directly affect them!*

Since I have refuted the "factors" that the authors claim "shaped current configurations of neighborhood based organizing," then their claim of community building being "spurred" as the dominant type of neighborhood organizing is also incorrect. It may be the preferred type as outlined by the city officials, urban planners, and others, but in the world of application and practicality, political activists are still about organizing small pockets of groups with similar interests and putting pressure on the status quo. It is about confidence-building, coalition-building, and consciousness-raising; if these are successful, *then you have the basis for a grass roots movement* – real community-building.

KEY: CONNECT COMMUNITY WORK WITH "RE-EDUCATION

One of the reasons for the success of the Triple One Neighborhood Association was the subsequent creation of the Triple One Parents' Union, which immediately went to the rescue of black students who were, on varying levels, being abused by the Omaha Public Schools.

The youth are our future and if we defend and develop them, we automatically pave the way for on-going progress. But it has to be done on a playing field that we control and/or have major input into. We have to be able to reject, in detail, defiance and self-determination, the vile and vulgar images and assertions imposed on us by the educational system. They can only teach what they know: and when it comes to cultural inclusion or relativity, they know very little.

Our young people – the students in this educational system - are also victims of stereotype-related maltreatment. **Racism then, perpetuates stigma.** A book titled *Crisis in Black and White* bought out some interesting points in 1964. The author, Charles Silberman, wrote,

> ... For one thing, the children become aware almost from infancy of the opprobrium Americans attach to color. They feel it in their parents' voices as they are warned to behave when they stray beyond the ghetto's wall. They become aware of it as they begin to watch television, or go to movies, or read the mass-circulation magazines; beauty, success, and status all wear a white skin. (Silberman, 1964: p. 48)

Although simplistic, it makes the point. These are issues that far too many of us do not discuss with our kids. When Triple One was going to meetings with teachers and school board members, the parents would be sitting right there, afraid to say much of anything. We had to be their voice because what the children were experiencing is the same thing, to a greater extent, that their parents had also faced when they went to school. And what was that, you ask?

> They learn to feel ashamed of their color as they learn to talk and thereby to absorb the invidiousness our very language attaches to color. White represents purity and goodness, black represents evil. The white lie is the permissible misstatement, the black lie the inexcusable falsehood; the black sheep is the one who goes astray (and when he goes astray, he receives a

black mark on his record); defeat is black (the stock market
crashed on "Black Thursday"), victory white ... (Silberman,
1964: pp. 49-50)

Therefore, to have power, we have to first of all gain power over our own minds and what we "feed" those minds. It is not enough to be in the community organizing while our children enter schools that feed them pablum about how great white people are. This would create conflict within our families and self-esteem issues in the hearts and actions of our future generations. That is why community work, a form of education in itself, has to nevertheless be connected with a "re-education" campaign because the battle for the minds of the people is, as Mao taught, the first half of the struggle.

At the core of community and neighborhood development issues are issues of differing perspectives on what is "good" for our communities. These differing definitions are based on race, and the racial differences are rooted in different types of symbolism. Again, Silberman:

The symbolism which elevates white and debases black
inevitably affects the consciousness of every person, white
or black ... This arrangement of things [is] communicated
to all in our culture by all its modes and means, passed by
osmosis through all the membrances of class, caste and
color of relationships, caressingly and painlessly injected
into our children by their school texts and, even more, their
story books ... (Silberman, 1964: p. 114)

Having been a graduate student in one of the top urban education programs in the nation at the University of Wisconsin-Milwaukee, I learned and studied a great deal about how to change the structure of American education. What they taught me is what I turned around and improved. It was what I learned creating the Triple One Parents Union and organizing in the Omaha community that I wrote about and used in my classroom debates, not the other way around.

At any rate, a key aspect of "re-education" is not only aimed at young people, but also at the teachers themselves – they must be "de-racicized:"

... teacher education that embraces an anti-racist perspective
recognizes that prospective teachers' and teachers'
sensibilities are shaped by the same forces that mold us in the
society at large ... However' antiracist educators understand
racism as learned behavior and, as such, it can be unlearned
(Ladson-Billings, 2000: 211).

These movements – working in the schools to change the teacher attitudes and the curriculum – can run concurrently with the work being done in the community, just as I did with the Triple One Neighborhood Association and then the Triple One Parents Union, later combining the names (and functions) to become TONAPU -- the Triple One Neighborhood Association and Parents Union.

KEY: DEFINE LEADERSHIP TYPES:
URBAN MODELS AS A BASIS FOR BLACK POLITICAL ACTION
A THEORY AND PROSPECTIVE PARADIGMS

There needs to be some standards for black leadership regardless of the region, the locality, the size of the area, the conditions of the constituency. Black men and women should be just that: "black." And I don't mean "black" in the negative connotation that the white man implies and applies. I mean "black" so that when you hear them speaking, the content of what they are saying clearly distinguishes them from white politicians and leaders, and that means that the solutions that they offer are tailor-made for us, rather than some generic, bland, "one-size-fits-all" strategy that they borrow from their white colleagues.

Since the death of Martin Luther King, Jr., black leadership has, for the most part, been a major disappointment. Some would say that they have been an abysmal failure. They have become to system-oriented, too self-absorbed, too greedy, to obsessed with getting on television or getting their name in the papers, and generally naïve of the issues other than those they glean or gather from the easily assembled facts of the oppressor.

This indictment fits all of them, from religious and civic leaders to political leaders and, in many cases, even the grass roots organizer types. Why these proposed urban models of black leadership? Simply, somebody has to do something. Some kind of standards have to be established so that, at very least, we will be able to see where these people are going, why they chose to lead, how they endeared themselves to the community, how they actually feel about black people (other than their friends and family members) and so on.

At present it seems that anyone can become a leader without actually having to be one. I've seen actual nitwits rise to the level of community wide observance in cities like Dallas, Milwaukee, and Omaha. And I've studied black leadership and their ideas and movements from the days of antebellum slavery up to the present. As a Black Studies scholar and instructor, I make it a point to know more about my history than any white man. As a result, I care more than most people because I've devoted myself to working toward digging us out of this rut that we've gotten ourselves in, mainly because of our police-dog like commitment to the concept of "integration."

Urban Models of Black Leadership, borrowing from three models of urban land use, may sound grandiose. But it gives us a starting point, especially since black people seem to hell-bent on following anybody any place out of some misplaced sense of racial loyalty. That approach worked back in the day when our leadership was accountable to us; that is no longer the case. They now pay homage to white people, money, being on the down-low, crack cocaine and a host of other secondary issues that take precedence over the long-term well-being of black folks. Next, a synopsis and overview of the three urban land use models.

The Three Models of Urban Land/Leadership: Explanation

As an Urban Studies/Urban Planning student (graduate school at the University of Nebraska Omaha and the University of Iowa) I enjoyed this field of study immensely. I learned a great deal about zoning, urban law and legislation, public economy, utilities and how they are determined, construction of streets, tax incremental financing and so much more. As one interview regarding the study of land use informs us:

The study of urban land use generally draws from three different descriptive models. These models were developed to generalize about the patterns of urban land use found in early industrial cities of the U.S. Because the shape and form of American cities changed over time, new models of urban land were developed to describe an urban landscape that was becoming increasingly complex and differentiated.

These models served as a basis for analysis, and were developed at different times. When placed together, they give urban planners a better understanding of city configurations. But nothing is perfect, and,

> … because these are general models devised to understand the overall patterns of land use, none of them can accurately describe patterns of urban land use in all cities. In fact, all of these models have been criticized for being more applicable to cities in the U.S. than to cities of other nations. Other criticisms have focused on the fact that the models are static; they describe patterns of urban land use in a generic city, but do not describe the process by which land use changes. Despite these criticisms, these models continue to be useful generalizations of the way in which land is devoted to different uses within the city. Below, we will examine the Concentric Zone Model, Sector Model and Multiple Nuclei Model of urban land use.

Criticism only serves to make future ideas stronger. This is why I believe that these three models serve as a necessary foundation for the development of what I call generically call "Community Leadership Paradigms" and, more specifically, Urban Models of Black Leadership. Here is why.

To begin with, these models will enable us to establish patterns on the part of those black leaders and those who aspire to lead. These patterns will provide far more stability than anything we have now because for the most part, black people simply refuse to judge or critique black leadership. In recent years, this has served to hurt us, since those who think that they have carte blanche have opted to ignore their constituencies and opt, instead, to carve their own personal niches in the system or seek out riches (or sexual gratification) in some other capacity.

Secondly, like the urban land models, the models of black leadership are more applicable to cities and towns in the U.S. than in other nations. This is not to imply that black leadership throughout the Diaspora cannot be bought off or controlled by outside interests. But the black leadership models that I offer here speak to the unique contradiction that their constituents as well as the majority of people in this country seem to buy into: that being that in America, anyone can "make it," we're all equal, and that all of us have opportunities. These lies, when placed in a real world context, point to many of the problems that black people face: we tend to believe in slogans, phrases, axioms, maxims and catch phrases even when we see the reality right in our face. This is how black leaders can get away with almost anything and yet continue to have large followings, constituencies, congregations and supporters.

Third, like the land use models, these black leaders are a static essence: they seem to act in the same way and there is no process by which their leadership changes or adapts to the needs of the people that they are leading. Almost all of them have Type A personalities and seem to bring with them a "my way or the highway" approach to leadership and community organizing. My models take this into account and do offer some suggestions that offer the masses of black people better options and alternatives when it comes to leadership selection.

Fourth, like the land use models, my models hopefully offer "useful generalizations" of ways in which black leadership assumes and claims to be, as well as what it actually is, when it comes to the defense and development of their followers/constituents/congregants.

In the following section we will examine the Sector Model, Multiple Nuclei Model and Concentric Zone models of urban land use where each will be immediately followed up with my definitions of Urban Community Leadership. Once you get an overview of what these three models are about, then it will easier to understand the leadership styles that I developed based upon the previously described land use urban planning paradigm.

The Three Models of Urban Land Use/Community Leadership

The first land use form is called the "concentric zone model." This will be explained and then the concept of The Concentric Zone Model Community Leadership Paradigm will be defined and elaborated upon.

Land Use: Concentric Zone

The first land use form is called the "concentric zone model." This will be explained and then the concept of The Concentric Zone Model Community Leadership Paradigm will be defined and elaborated upon.

Envision with me, if you will, a target, with the bull's eye in the middle and rings, white and black, surrounding that bull's eye. This is what the concentric zone model looks like: a central business district in the middle and then a ring around it consisting of neighborhoods, a ring around that consisting of services and then the outer rings, consisting of the suburbs and exurbs. Specifically, Burgess identified five rings of land use that would form around the CBD. These rings were originally defined as the (1) central business district, (2) zone of transition, (3) zone of independent workers' homes, (4) zone of better residences and (5) zone of commuters. An important feature of this model is the positive correlation of socio-economic status of households with distance from the CBD -- more affluent households were observed to live at greater distances from the central city The model was based on Burgess's observations of Chicago during the early years of the 20th century. Major routes of transportation emanated from the city's core, making the CBD the most accessible location in the city.

The Concentric Zone Community Leadership Paradigm

This is the model that describes Omaha the best out of the three in terms of geo-spatial arrangement. It is also the model that offers the potential to be the most far-reaching in terms of political and socioeconomic scope as it relates to the other populations across the city and even the state. However, as a leadership paradigm, I designed something that has never been considered, but if it was, the black community of North Omaha (conceptualized here as our "central business district") would have optimal and far-reaching leadership that would be diverse socioeconomically, but unified in terms of the collective agreement that North

Omaha has to be the focus and fulcrum of attention, resource development and real empowerment.

Two representatives from the four outer rings would be a part of the **Concentric Council of Elders**, a total of eleven representatives (including three from the CBD) that would serve as the guiding/governmental body of the Concentric Zone Community Leadership Paradigm.

With North Omaha as our CBD (central "leadership" district), what each ring surrounding the area would represent would be supportive networks functioning, generally, in leadership specific capacities that, in turn, feed into the CBD thereby empowering and strengthening North Omaha (the CBD).

Directly surrounding and contiguous to the CBD is our **zone of transition**, an area where young leaders that we would be mentored – an area of protégés, close enough to the CBD but serving as a *"learning layer"* that would also be able to deal with the more stable leadership in the next sector. Two leaders from this area sit on the Concentric Council of Elders that serves as the governing body of the centrally located CBD. Mentored by all of the other zones, including the CBD, this is the zone that represents the future leaders of the paradigm.
In other words, this zone of transition would be responsible for learning all they could from the CBD, but also circulating and disseminating information about history, culture, economics, law and other areas, not only within their zone of transition, but also to the third ring of leaders, known herein as "the zone of independent thinkers' homes."

The **zone of independent thinkers** is made up of the intelligentsia, the brain trust for the community. Two leaders from this area sit on the Concentric Council of Elders that serves as the governing body of the centrally located CBD. The zone of independent thinkers is just that: working in the traditional system outside of the community but committing itself to work toward development of the CBD, while also mentoring the protégés from the "learning layer" previously decribed (zone of transition).

In addition to the zone of transition and the zone of independent thinker's homes, we have the **zone of logistics**. Two leaders from this area sit on the Concentric Council of Elders that serves as the governing body of the centrally located CBD.

The zone of logistics is where the well-to-do members of the black community live, meaning that they have the financial wherewithal to host important meetings and fundraisers to finance the projects aimed at improving the CBD. These are the economic entities that plough monies into whatever is needed by the protégés, the independent workers and, of course, the CBD proper. That is why they are "independent"; they may work in the system but they don't necessarily have to. Because of their financial status, they might be corporate directors or living on an inheritance; at any rate, their location and status serve as a buffer against incursions from the majority community (both financially and physically) and again, they don't have to worry about "retaliation" from an employer or harassment by police because they are system-oriented "negroes" who have the best interests of the CBD and its residents at heart.

Finally is the **mobility zone** (known in urban planning as the zone of commuters). These would be the individuals who would be in charge of "diaspora relations," meaning that black people, no matter where they lived in Nebraska, would be recruited and incorporated into the expansion and beautification of the CBD (North Omaha). Two leaders from this area sit on the Concentric Council of Elders that serves as the governing body of the centrally located CBD. This is the zone where people live who are retired or independently wealthy, many hailing from and regularly interacting with the residents of the zone of logistics.

To recap: we have North Omaha as the central business district; then there is the zone of transition on the inner ring contiguous to the CBD, the zone of independent thinkers, the zone of logistics and finally, on the outer ring, the mobility zone. This then, is the substance and structure of the Concentric Zone Community Leadership Model.

Land Use: Sector Model

Sector model is when the city is cut into different "sections" and the central business district is located somewhere in the middle. Soon after Burgess generalized about the concentric zone form of the city, Homer Hoyt, while recognizing the value of the concentric ring model, also observed some consistent patterns in many American cities. He observed, for example, that it was common for low-income households to be found in close proximity to railroad lines, and commercial establishments to be found along business thoroughfares. In 1939, Hoyt modified the concentric zone model to account for major transportation routes.

Recall that most major cities evolved around the nexus of several important transport facilities such as railroads, sea ports, and trolly lines that eminated from the city's center. Recognizing that these routes (and later metropolitan expressways and interstate highways) represented lines of greater access, Hoyt theorized that cities would tend to grow in wedge-shaped patterns, or sectors, eminating from the CBD and centered on major transportation routes. Higher levels of access translate to higher land values. Thus, many commercial functions would remain in the CBD, but manufcaturing activity would develop in a wedge surrounding transport routes.

The Sector Model Community Leadership Paradigm

Transportation routes also serve a key role in the Sector Model Community Leadership Paradigm that I propose. Recall that Hoyt noticed that it was common for low-income households to be found in close proximity to railroad lines, and commercial establishments to be found along business thoroughfares. Black communities are always plagued and divided by some type of railroad tracks; the belief in the '60s was that this was so that if the community had to be divided or trapped, trains could be bought in to do just that.

Just as Hoyt accounted for major transportation routes, North Omaha could do the same thing. Whose community has trucks travelling through it all times of night? Whose community has the concentration of the Metro Area Transit bus routes (and the pollution that it brings)? Whose community has proximity to the river which, in turn, has the potential for the creation of shipping docks for exporting our goods to other parts of the state and region?

Recall also that Hoyt theorized that cities would tend to grow in wedge-shaped patterns, or sectors, emanating from the CBD and centered on major transportation routes. But here is the key: many commercial functions would remain in the CBD, but manufacturing activity would develop in a wedge surrounding transport routes. And this is where the positive productions of what I am proposing is given form and function in terms of leadership

We develop the businesses in North Omaha and bring back the people to improved housing, but use various parts of north Omaha (northeast, east, southwest and the western fringe as out-going (and incoming)transportation routes.
The leadership would function the same way, with the main "sector" being the heart of North Omaha that would be re-named "New Kemet." Kmet is what Egypt was called before the name change, and it translates to mean "land of the blacks." Because of residential and racial segregation in Milwaukee, that is what the central city was – the land of the blacks.

At the basis of my proposed Sector Model Community Leadership Paradigm would be our own City Charter. The preamble, which I developed using Omaha's city charter as a basis, would go like this:

> WE, THE PEOPLE, citizens of Omaha and residents of
> the inner city, In order to form a more symbiotic set of
> relations, increase the prospects for mutual benefit,
> ensure internal stability, increase the area's tranquility,
> provide for common defense and development, promote
> the general welfare of each other, and secure the
> blessings of liberation to ourselves and our Posterity, do
> ordain and seek to establish, maintain and enhance the

existence of the area of Omaha known hereafter as NEW KEMET.

The Sector Model Community Leadership Paradigm has three leaders of each of the proposed four (4) sectors (northeast, east, southwest and the western fringe) with three representatives from the CBD (North Omaha) for *a Sector Model Strategic Commission* total of 15 persons. The western fringe is bounded by 90th Street on the west, extending from the southwest side to the northwest side.

Every quarter, one of the sectors outside of the CBD hosts a *Strategic Commission Conference* that is open to everyone from the community, with emphasis on each conference revolving around an agenda of items peculiar to that sector. For instance, conference would take place in March, June, September and December. Each conference would address issues of leadership and fundraising with emphasis on empowering North Omaha.

Land Use: Multiple Nuclei

The third and final land use form is called the "multiple nuclei model." This will be explained and then the concept of The Multiple Nuclei Community Leadership Paradigm will be defined and elaborated upon.
In the multiple nuclei model, the city consists of several different areas and as such, there may be more than one business district to serve these various areas.
By 1945, it was clear to Chauncy Harris and Edward Ullman that many cities did not fit the traditional concentric zone or sector model. Cities of greater size were developing substantial suburban areas and some suburbs, having reached significant size, were functioning like smaller business districts. These smaller business districts acted as satellite nodes, or nuclei, of activity around which land use patterns formed.

For instance if we were to use Omaha (which is not typical), the nuclei would be Millard, LaVista, Ralston, Council Bluffs, Papillion and Bellevue. As Harris and Ullman stated, the CBD still exists, but specialized cells of activity would develop according to specific requirements of certain activities, different rent-paying abilities, and the tendency for some kinds of economic activity to cluster together.

The Multiple Nuclei Community Leadership Paradigm

This leadership paradigm develops North Omaha as a collection of "neighborhoods" or "villages" that would be directed by key individuals/representatives. The CBD, in this case, would be 30th and Ames Streets.

The area would be divided into the following five (5) "multiple nuclei:" 68102-east/downtown, 68111-central, 68131-southcentral, 68104-northwest, and 68110-northeast. The leadership directory would consist of three individuals from each of the five nuclei and six from the CBD, for a total of 21 directors.

Each of the areas has more than one business district, which would serve to empower the area with each nucleus working alongside the other four to engage in cooperative buying power and collective fund-raising ventures. Around each business district in each area will be: small parking lots, dotted with apartments and condos, housing surrounding each of these areas and on the outer area, heavy industrial. This offers the potential for close proximity to jobs, cutting down on commute times and addressing the lack of transportation problems that plagues North Omaha (the CBD).

An annual event would be the North Omaha Black Businessmen's Bazaar, with all five areas involve in the planning and implementation. Other collective events on the part of the multiple nuclei would include: (1) the Multiple Nuclei Concert Series; (2) the Multiple Nuclei Lobby, which would include leadership sitting in on the Community Development Block Grant planning sessions, no longer merely responding to the allocations once the decisions have been made; (3) the Multiple Nuclei Education Symposium and (4) the Multiple Nuclei Health and Legal Forums.

NATIONAL LEAGUE OF CITIES

"The people that elect corrupt politicians, impostors, thieves and traitors are not victims. They are accomplices."

--George Orwell

Five years ago the leeches that call themselves city leadership latched onto another empty effort that was geared toward "comprehensive African-American Male Achievement." Following is what was promised in 2013, what actually happened, and my expert analysis of both.

Under the caption, "Omaha one of 11 Cities selected for comprehensive African-American Male Achievement Initiative," the website announcement begins thusly:

> In 2013, the National League of Cities with the support of the Open Society Foundation and PolicyLink **created an eleven city cohort referred to as the Black Male Achievement Initiative**. During the spring of 2013, **the Empowerment Network and City of Omaha made an application to the National League of Cities to become part of their Black Male Achievement Initiative.** Omaha was notified in May

> of 2013 that it was one of 11 cities selected to move forward **with a technical assistance grant** to develop a comprehensive plan focused on the success of African-American boys and young men in Omaha. **The Empowerment Network Collaboration, a seven year nationally recognized initiative,** includes all of these goals and has active collaborations and measurable results in each area identified as priorities by the National League of Cities. (City of Omaha Press Conference, 2014 – emphasis added)

To begin with, if you have an "African-American Empowerment" component to the larger and resource-rich Empowerment Network, then why the need to apply for the Black Male Achievement Grant? Wasn't black male achievement a part of what the Black empowerment component pledged to do, along with 100 Black Men and Black Men United. Have they moved the demographic needle for black families (other than their own) one notch since they formed? No.

Secondly, the year is now 2018 and there has been only negligible attention paid to the plight of black boys other than to keep locking them up. This so-called collaboration holds meetings and feeds people, but the thrust of any social activism continues to still be limited to prayer vigils. The political leadership is invisible on the issue. Remember: this is year five of a seven year initiative.

The information continues:

> **Mayor Jean Stothert agreed to continue the city's participation with the initiative in partnership with the Empowerment Network** and assigned Cameron Gales and Barb Farho as the cities representatives. Willie Barney, President and Facilitator of the Empowerment Network, is the **community leader** and facilitator. One of the requirements for the NLC initiative is **the active involvement of elected officials** as stakeholders. (City of Omaha Press conference, 2014)

One has to ask that with so little activity and with the people involved being almost invisible for the past five years, were the INTENTIONS of those who submitted this grant request even remotely "honorable"? With the lax involvement it appears to be more like yet another example of Omaha scamming the government out of money in the name of the poor, getting the assistance and then squandering it. Large meetings, festivals and short-term bullshit programs that yield literally nothing appear to be the order of the day. When you see who the "political leaders" are who are involved, you will be better able to see why this is the case:

> The Omaha project includes a number of elected officials including African-American leaders: City Councilmen Ben Gray and Franklin

> Thompson; Douglas County Commissioner Chris Rodgers; Douglas
> County Treasurer John Ewing; School Board Members Justin Wayne,
> Marque Snow and Yolanda Williams. The focus of the initiative is five-
> fold: strengthening African-American families; improving educational
> outcomes; improving access to quality health care; connecting AA young
> men and men to employment; and reducing involvement in
> violence.(City of Omaha Press conference. 2014)

Can there be any wonder why, for five years, none of these people has been seen anywhere near where the majority of those black boys live, and that is north Omaha?

Ben Gray is an elected official and his effectiveness is dubious, at best. In fact, he headed an African American Achievement team of the Omaha Public Schools and not only did it fall flat on its face, but the students actually ended up doing worse. The best he could come up with was a "greeter program" where black men lined up and shook hands with black students as they entered a particular school each morning. Have grades improved? No. Have expulsions and suspensions of black students decreased? No. Like this Black Male Initiative, it is all smoke and mirrors and looking back at it every time you see an application for a grant filled with promises, pledges and bullshit, the grant arrives and white folks get together with a few negro lackeys and "cut up the money." The kids don't see any cash, only chicken wings, potato salad, sandwiches from Jimmy Johns and maybe a few plaques.

Franklin Thompson ran for office in a suburban district and won twice. That speaks volumes. He was recently appointed to head the feckless Human Rights Department which is a part of the city administration in name only. His most recent act of ignorance was referring to 500 refugees from Myanmar who were evacuated from a roach- and bed bug-infested apartment complex as being better off than they were in "the Third World." Third World is as big an insult as when President Trump referred to Haiti and African nations as "shit hole countries."

Chris Rodgers is a perennial representative on the Douglas County Board who is known for failing at jobs, being taken off of them and given chances elsewhere. The only reason he hasn't been replaced on the Douglas County Board is because it is an elected position. He knows nothing about black people or North Omaha and carries on the tradition of non-activity left to him by his predecessor, Carole Woods-Harris.

John Ewing is a former cops and a Johnny-come-lately, hardly even known or recognized by any black youth. The same goes for his wife who held a position with the Omaha Housing Authority and with another one of his relatives who serves as director of the Great Plains Black Museum. As the former interim director of that museum (4-1/2 years) and of the Plano African American Museum,

I can say in all seriousness that putting this Ewing guy in charge of Nebraska's black history is like handing a blond over to the Creature from the Black Lagoon. Destruction will loom.

Justin Wayne is no longer a school board member but is just as impotent as a member of the Nebraska Legislature. Another confused mulatto who has to read any views he has about the black community. His ignorance of black Omaha is incredibly evident. Marque Snow is a black member of the gay community which explains his role conflict related issues, and Yolanda Williams moved to a more suburban setting and willingly relinquished her seat on the school board.

What a collection! Of what, I have no idea.

<u>The Promises of the "Community Partners</u>

Next come the promised goals of the "community partners" who collectively, failed and continue to fail miserably – as has been their decades long track record when it comes to "helping" the black community or, more specifically, "black girls" and "black boys." My analyses will filter in and out between each of the "agreements" (pledges) that are offered.

Here is what is described in terms of the planning that went into it. I will present their strategy and then comment on each variable on the other side:

The planning team worked with a group of community partners during the summer of 2013 to develop an initial action plan which was submitted to the National League of Cities to qualify for a year of additional technical assistance. As a part of the process, over 40 representatives from various entities worked on the plan, and 20 signed letters of intent and agreed to participate formally to:

1. ENGAGE IN PLANNING WITH OTHER STAKEHOLDERS
2. PARTICIPATE WITHIN AN AGREED UPON STRUCTURE
3. COLLECT AND SHARE DATA
4. ALIGN STRATEGIES AS PART OF A COMPREHENSIVE PLAN
5. ACTIVELY ENGAGE YOUTH IN DECISION-MAKING

Now, over 50 organizations have agreed to participate with the plan as it continues to move forward and others are joining in each month. The group has also hosted two community meetings to gather additional ideas and recommendations for the strategies.(City of Omaha Press Conference, 2014)

To learn more about the Omaha African-American Male Achievement Collaborative or to get involved with this initiative, please click here.

Where or where to begin? Even the racist Buffalo Bill Cody got it right when he once said, "Every Indian outbreak that I have ever known has resulted from broken promises and broken treaties by the government." And the same can be said for the promises made on these grants applied for and received by the City of Omaha. The only difference is that the quote would be "Every on-going bout of impoverishment that grows in North Omaha has resulted from broken promises and broken pledges by the City of Omaha (and the State of Nebraska).'

Now for the analysis of the previously listed "plan".

They begin with the claim of a "planning team" consisting of community partners during the summer of 2013 that developed an "initial action plan" that was then submitted to the National League of Cities. Who wrote it? Who was the brains of the outfit? Have debated and defeated the best minds of white people throughout college and on through graduate school I know what takes place when they form these "committees." What they do is find out who the expert and writer among them is and then use that individual to springboard off of, dole out the major components of the assignment to, develop and write the framework and vision and then some white girl does the typing and they all place their names on it, usually with the mayor's name going on top.

This is not what I view as a collective effort and is the major reason why I don't like working in groups. All the work gets done by an "active minority" and everyone else lies, goes to the bar and claims to their wives, girlfriends and boyfriends that they are "working on a major project." This sounds impressive, but most of them couldn't outline the executive summary of the project or the outcomes if they were forced to. Not only that, but Omaha's leadership does not consist of people who are the sharpest knives in the drawer. You can just watch them during television interviews and news snippets to immediately find that out.

Forty representatives from various "entities" (not organizations) worked on the plan. How were they selected? This is how bias creeps in. It's usually the same old "buddy System," the same coterie of individuals who are greedy grant seekers who clone other reports, plagiarize sections out of other draft proposals and then immediately and expeditiously put together something that they believe looks impressive. Add that to a lazy governmental entity – in this case the National League of Cities – and you have the perfect storm of redundancy, cultural ignorance and classic examples of "reinventing the wheel."

There are five areas that this "team of partners" combined to work on that are worthy of critique and commentary. I shall go through each of them. Twenty signed letters of intent from these committee members agreed to do the following:

1. <u>ENGAGE IN PLANNING WITH OTHER STAKEHOLDERS</u>

When Omaha speaks of "stakeholders" they are talking about white people who have been informed ahead of time about the "stakes" involved. That is how these organizations, committees, and groups consistently remain comprised of the same people, the same types, the same corporate background and the same ideological and cultural backwardness.

When these groups remain of the same type and stripe, the product is a reflection of what has come before. Their thinking is so limited and homogenous that what goes in is what comes out. The idea of "stakeholders" sounds good on paper, but in reality few people understand what a stakeholder is. The dictionary definition is, "a person or group that has an investment, share, or interest in something, as a business or industry." The key terms are "share" and "interest" which means some type of investment. And that investment is either directly or indirectly financial.

Examples are like when they order signage for a project. It is their white associates who get the contracts. When they have a community event, it is their buddies who own the fast food restaurants who get the contracts. There are no bids that are letted; there is no information disseminated that would promote input from outside and more culturally divergent forces and sources. No: the stakeholders are of the same thought process and as such, work to maintain an kind of "in-house" approach to whatever it is they are engaged in.

In this case, a proposal for black males. These white men and women convince themselves that they know what is best for black people when the only black people they work around are of the "house negro" variety, all powerless, and all more than willing to tow the corporate line. In simpler terms, at the "planning table" are whites who have power and a token sprinkling of people of color who work for those people who have the power.

So they agreed to hang out, drink, cavort, party and engage in social intercourse with people that they already know. In other words, a clique.

2. PARTICIPATE WITHIN AN AGREED UPON STRUCTURE

These people then agreed that they would participate in an agreed upon structure that THEY helped to formulate. How difficult can that be when what they have produced is but a repeat of what has been "formulated" before? That is how Omaha remains so staid and stoic, so locked in place. Despite desperate attempts to appear urbane and "metropolitan," these are hillbillies in Halsten; hicks in high heels; clods decked out in Hart, Schaffner and Marx. And they have to know it because not only do they work together and drink together but they live near each other in gated communities.

Working within an agreed upon structure also ensures limited cultural input or new ideas entering into the "clique." It will be the same ol' same ol' and in that way both the process and the product can be controlled from within. To show the collective ignorance of the group, not a single one views this criteria as being even remotely problematic. To this homogeneous group, this myopic and one-race way of developing an idea for nonwhites is the way "things are supposed to be."

3. COLLECT AND SHARE DATA

This particular component of the "plan" can be undertaken and completed by a single individual, two or three at most. Working with black males is nothing more than a data collection tactic, a data bank compiling information on "the undesirables." What will be done with it? The Omaha Police Division tried to conduct a mandatory DNA sampling several years ago before it was halted by State Senator Ernie Chambers so the point here is that the River City's leadership is not above compiling data on its citizens, especially those citizens that don't look like the majority population members.

And this goes back to the interlocking directorates that rule Omaha. Back in the late '70s/early '80s black people were applying for and receiving arts grants from different sources around the city. The first move made to squash this was to eliminate the Metropolitan Arts Council. Then came the consolidation of the corporations and the interlocking directorates. Third came the "prioritization" of the big five arts groups: opera Omaha, the Omaha symphony, the Nebraska Arts Council, and several others. All white, all given priority.

The same takes place among nonprofits, with the nonwhite numbers dwindling every day. The paltry and pitiful input by people of color in Omaha's black leadership ranks is brutally embarrassing. The Black Studies Department at UNO (not that it would make a major difference) is rarely consulted. Only negroes from the Urban League of Nebraska, the Omaha NAACP, the Omaha Economic Development Corporation (OEDC) and new arrivals that work for Susie Buffett are ever deemed fit for "negro input." The city's Human Relations Department is a front, a shill and a façade to give the illusion that people have an advocate against discrimination.

4. ALIGN STRATEGIES AS PART OF A COMPREHENSIVE PLAN

How can you "align strategies" that are all clones of one another when it comes to the outcomes of those strategies? People who are limited in scope cannot create something that is "comprehensive" other than that which falls within their purview. These Omaha leaders don't have an international scope other than when it has something to do with farming. They are sorely lacking in cultural competence and have to run to the Minnesota Humanities Council for "cultural advocacy manuals" and other "tips on the coloreds" in order to get even a partial hold on the idea of multicultural content and focus.

To be comprehensive means "to cover completely or broadly." If Omaha leadership had the capacity to do this, the present-day racial and residential segregation and rampant job, housing and health discrimination would not exist. To even make such a statement as one of the components of this plan is a lie, an insult and a joke.

5. ACTIVELY ENGAGE YOUTH IN DECISION-MAKING

How are you going to "actively engage youth" in decision-making? Of course: you will assign the "negroes" on the committee to go out and "fetch" some black males to come in and babble about what they need and want, and what will it come down to? "Mo' money, mo' food, mo' recreation. All of which is consumable, akin to Toys for Tots and Coats for Kids. Once these consumables run out, poverty can therefore be maintained and as such, Omaha will continue to qualify for future federal grants such as Community Service Block Grants and Community Development Block Grants.

Here is how this "plan" closes out:

> Now, over **50 organizations have agreed to participate with the plan as it continues to move forward and others are joining in each month**. The group has also hosted two community meetings to gather additional ideas and recommendations for the strategies.(City of Omaha Press Conference, 2014 – emphasis added)

How many is "over 50 organizations"? Why can't they say? This may sound petty but it is quite indicative of the camouflaged commentary, the veiled lies that you get in a written document or a verbal pledge from these "Omaha leaders," be they black or white. One need only study the record because as Malcolm X taught, "Of all our studies, history is best qualified to reward our research."

Just look at the lies these people tell in the name of a plan. This is a historical habit, a repetitive ritual. Simply take this case of the National League of Cities program. What I just shared was committed in 2014. Here we are in 2018. Has the plight or predicament of black males improved at all? No. Have these leaders been more visible in the black community? No. Only the city councilman shows up after a shooting or some other controversy such as the evacuation of the Yale Apartments. This is not leadership.

Quotes From the May 15, 2014 Press Conference

Promises. Promises. And few if any are ever kept, especially when the subject has to do with Black Omahans. The following set of statements comes from a website and appears under the heading, "Quotes from the May 15, 2014 Press Conference. Following are those quotes, the people who made them, and my realistic interpretation of each of them.

We begin with the Mayor's pledge:

"We want to thank the National League of Cities and PolicyLink for the opportunity to partner on this great initiative. The city of Omaha, Empowerment Network and over 40 partners have created this collaborative. … We have the partnerships that will lead us to success."
– Mayor Jean Stothert – City of Omaha

There you have that dynamic duo of control: the City of Omaha and the Empowerment Network. The "partners" are various types that one or the other of these controls directly or indirectly. You have a white woman who is the city's political leader and another blond who is the daughter of one of the world's richest women. Neither of them knows a thing about the black community or urban planning and none of the "negroes" who they have under their supervision could hold a candle to me in a debate on either subject. And yet here they are. Triple One is the largest black neighborhood group in the city but these Anglos pick and choose who they feel comfortable with. That is another reason why black males in the city suffer: in order for black males to receive help, white females have to feel "secure."

The next quote from from a representative of the National League of Cities:

"Omaha scored extremely high on what they were currently doing and what they proposed to do. …We will lift up Omaha as being on the forefront in this work. … We're excited to see the partnerships between the city and community."
– Leon Andrews – National League of Cities

This is not the first roll in the hay between the City of Omaha and the Nation League of Cities. When former Mayor Hal Daub formed another farcical commission in 1997, this one on "race," it was the National League of Cities that was quoted in the document's introduction. Let me refresh your memory.

As I wrote in my analysis of that "race committee" back in 1997 (over two decades ago) "this document is an exercise in futility, and starts off with what I view as "grandiose quotes" by the League of Cities."

"The first such quote, from the 1991 League of Cities document, titled, "Diversity and Governance," reads as follows: "The first requirement of city leaders is that they embrace diversity and affirm equal rights for all. From that there can be no retreat." This is not true. City leaders need to ACT on that which has already been confirmed by law and by God. Their affirmation is unnecessary if they would but just act."

"On the same page is another quote, this one from "Building a Nation of Communities," also by the League of Cities: "Deep-seated problems such as racism, economic exclusion, and a sense of political powerlessness often stand in the way of residents feeling they have a equal stake in their communities' success."

"Often stand in the way"? Are there times when racism, economic exclusion and a sense of political powerlessness WORK for people of color, or anyone else, for that matter? This statement, by being quoted, is a case of the blind leading the blind. This proves that what white people (and their Negro lackeys) find relevant, black people feel the opposite about."

To ensure balance, no doubt, there are two more quotes from the League of cities, the 1999 Futures Report. The question at the top of the page asks, "How Can We Undo Racism?" The first answer is "By Changing Ourselves," and the explanation reads,

> On the one hand, working against racism means changing what we, as individuals and elected leaders, are doing to keep racism alive – for example, by separating ourselves, intentionally or not, from individuals of different races, or by not speaking up when those around us make racist comments. (National League of Cities)

The question is, why haven't white folks done it? The answer is, because they cannot. As Dr. Frances Welsing teaches, racism is a matter of genetic survival for those people. If they fraternize and have sex, the product is a child of color. For their own survival on this planet, they must shield themselves from the brown gene, which is both sociogenically and genetically more powerful than the "white" gene.

The second answer is, "By Changing our Policies and Institutions," and the quote says:

> Dismantling racism also means changing the policies and the social and institutional systems that allow racism to remain an oppressive force – for example, by enabling police to stop motorists because of the color of their skin or by permitting banks to treat loan applicants of different races differently. (National League of Cities)

With these generic truisms out of the way (which provides evidence that the National League of Cities has no real understanding of or plan for urban reality or issues of race), the issue of the blind leading the blind continues with the quote regarding this "Black Male Initiative" of 2014.

According to this most recent quote, "Omaha scored extremely high on what they were currently doing and what they proposed to do." And exactly what was that? What is Omaha scoring high on other than telling lies to people who know nothing about Omaha? How can Omaha score high on areas that have to do with a black male initiative when the black males that they rely on don't have a clue about the history of black people, North Omaha or race relations? In other words, the National League of Cities is a rubber stamp. That was 21 years ago – now here they are issuing resource grants and guess who gets one: the same city that the League lied about in decades past.

Who are they therefore to "lift up Omaha as being on (sic) the forefront in this work." Based on what? Then the League concludes, "We're excited to see the partnerships between the city and community." Which "partnerships" were used as examples and then submitted to the League? A partnership consists of individuals. What have those individuals done that could convince an outside agency that these individuals, having formed a partnership, can get the job done? This is nothing but another scam, another set of lies because here we are four years into the initiative and nothing visible has been done thus far.

One of their "negro leaders," the leader of the Empowerment Network, speaks in general terms because he has no specifics. Check out his blabbering testimony:

"Our young men are resilient, brilliant and creative, they have incredible talent. …Our job is to make sure they have every opportunity possible to reach their full potential."
– Willie Barney, President and Facilitator of the Empowerment Network

You've heard these platitudes time and time again, from describing young athletes and students to graduating inmates and military cadets. They mean nothing unless you can point to something that these "young men" have actually produced. Without that all you have are the claims of Willie Barney, hardly an ideal prototype of a conscious black man. He has "empowered" no one because black people are not allowed to have access to real power. That is a national and local fact.

There are no guarantees other than that these young men who are supposed to be so brilliant and creative are going to have a chance (that's what an opportunity is) to reach their potential. They already have that chance based on their own so-called resilience, don't they? How is this initiative going to offer that which already exists? Why don't they offer them something more than "an opportunity"? Because they can't, that's why.

The black community's elected member of the city council is "next man up" as he offers the following claim:

"Once we provide hope, all other things are possible. Thank you to all the stake-holders. Stay in our lanes. Stay focused. Continue to collaborate. We have the talent to solve these problems and we will get it done."
– Councilman Ben Gray

As usual, air sandwiches. Hope without a plan is nothing but a dream. If that's the case, then how can "all other things be possible"? Hope is no kind of foundation you can use unless you add to it courage, conviction, intelligence and a goal – none of which is being offered by Gray or any of his croneys. He is about setting limits, not goals. That can be said in his claim to "stay in our lanes." That means "know your place," like white folks told us back during the days of slavery. He says, "Continue to collaborate." In other words work with the people who were a part of the problem all the time. Then he comes out of left field with the ecologically flawed conclusion that "We have the talent to solve these problems and we will get it done." This is Ben Gray's third term, nine years, and there is nothing that shows he has even a clue about what to do for or with young black males. There is no way he would ever debate me on this subject.

Another African-American city councilman (at that time) represented a white district (which speaks volumes). He has a doctorate in education but you notice the title of "doctor" is omitted. Following is what he had to say:

"The answer is bi-partisan… one political party cannot carry the weight. … these are not North Omaha's kids; these are Omaha's kids. If we're going to be suc-cessful, it's going to take people from both parties. …I believe Omaha will be the model city for the rest of nation."
– Councilman Franklin Thompson

These are outright misconceptions mixed with lies. It is clear that no political party is going to carry weight because both are overwhelmingly white. These are not "Omaha's kids." They belong to North Omaha because the city is segregated and segregation is a social statement that says, "They're not with me!" Omaha didn't even want these kids going to their schools and spent in excess of $300,000 fighting the order to desegregate and didn't desegregate until 1976 – 22 years after Brown v. Board of Education!

Thompson, who is now the director of the Human Rights Department for the City of Omaha (appointed by Republican mayor Stoethert) concludes with the claim, "I believe Omaha will be the model city for the rest of nation." Here we are four years in: where is Thompson's evidence? Omaha has NEVER been a model for anything other than how to control and abuse black people and how to lead the nation in black child poverty. Thompson lied, which is par for the course because the entire proposal submitted to the League of Cities was packed with lies.

CONCLUSION

These then, are the "keys" to empowerment – past and present - and they will lead to real empowerment, not the "flunkies fronting as formulators" type of empowerment that is taking place in and around Omaha at the present time. These individuals should actually be ashamed of themselves to have allowed these zany ideas, Neanderthal notions, hack-neyed clichés and foolish conclusions to have ever been put in print. Now their words, lack of insight and abysmal ignorance of race relations and cultural competency are in plain view for their progeny to see.
And so is this book.

REFERENCES

Biga, L. (____). Power players, Ben Gray and other Omaha African-American leaders try improvement through self-empowered networking. **The Reader.**

Edney, H.T. (2004, March 2). Presidential candidates understate extent of poverty. ***The Final Call.***

Fraser, J. & Kick, E. (2005). Understanding community building in urban America. **Journal of Poverty**, 9, (1). 23-43.

Fredericks, S. (2005, June 5). The uninsured in Omaha have "hope." Retrieved from http://www.hopemed.us/news/press_releases/uninsured.asp

Gibbons, Frederick X. "Stigma and Interpersonal Relationships" in Stephen C. Ainlay, Gaylene Becker and Lerita M. Coleman (Eds.) **The Dilemma of Difference: A Multidisciplinary View of Stigma.** New York: Plenum Press. 1986. Ladson-Billings, G.J. (2000, May/June). Fighting for our lives: Preparing teachers to teach African students. **Journal of Teacher Education**, 51.

Omaha Monitor. (1928, December 14). A city of homes.

Levy, John M. (2000). **Contemporary Urban Planning**. Upper Saddle River, New Jersey: Prentice-Hall.

Omaha World Herald (2004, December 13). Interracial barometer: A horrendous assault brings reminder of decline in one type of racial bigotry.

Omaha World Herald. (2002, July 22). Despite gains, blacks far from parity with whites, report says.

Silberman, Charles E. (1964). **Crisis in Black and White**. New York: Vintage Books.

Stelly, Matthew C. (2017, May) **A Sociological and Historical Overview Race Relations and the Omaha Public School: Documentation and Discussion.** North Charleston, South Carolina: Create Space publishers.

Stelly, Matthew C. (2017, May) **Homage to Omaha's Northside: Chronology, Critique, Commentary, Correction. Mindset 1, Volume I. Coloreds and Caucasians in Cornhusker Country.** North Charleston, South Carolina: CreateSpace Publishers.

Stelly, Matthew C. (2017, May). **Homage to Omaha's North Side: Chronology, Critique, Commentary, Correction: Mindset 2, Volume II In Defense of North Omaha: A Socially Corrective Critique of Adam Fletcher Sasse's "North Omaha History."** North Charleston, South Carolina: CreateSpace Publishers.

Stelly, Matthew C. (2018). **Urban Planning, Community Development and the Systematic Abuse of African- American Communities:: Contextual Appraisal, Commentary and Critique.** North Charleston, South Carolina: CreateSpace Publishers.

Stelly, Matthew C. (2018). **Mayors, Developers and the Manipulation of American Cities: The Economics and Sociopolitical Realities of Segregation of American Cities.** North Charleston, South Carolina.

Stelly, Matthew C. (2018). **Detrimental Reliance: Empowerment Movement, City Administration and North Omaha.** North Charleston, South Carolina.

Stelly, Matthew C. (2018) **Introduction to Africentric Sociourban Planning:: Concepts and Characteristics.** North Charleston, South Carolinad